From the Garden to the Table

To our children Adam, Freya and Tom

The Lyons Press is an imprint of The Globe Pequot Press.

First published by The Lyons Press 2003.

First published in 1999 under the title *Fork to Fork* by Conran Octopus Ltd, a part of Octopus Publishing Group Ltd.,
2-4 Heron Quays, Docklands, London E14 4JP.

ISBN 1-58574-628-2

Printed in Hong Kong

10 9 8 7 6 5 4 3 2 1

Library of Congress Cataloging-in-Publication data is available on file.

From the Garden to the Table

Monty and Sarah Don

Photography by Simon Wheeler

THE LYONS PRESS
Guilford, Connecticut
An imprint of The Globe Pequot Press

CONTENTS

INTRODUCTION

WHY BOTHER, AS THE THIRD MILLENNIUM BEGINS, to go to the trouble and expense of growing food in your garden? It is much cheaper and easier for all but the most remote household to travel to the nearest supermarket than to grow your own vegetables or fruit. The development of refrigerated transport and storage and the massed economies of scale have brought a range of fruit and vegetables to every Western home that only the most widely traveled person could have experienced as recently as my own childhood. Seasonal restrictions have been abolished. You can now as easily eat strawberries in January as you can oranges in July. A shopping basket now reflects what the shopper wishes to eat and can pay for rather than what is readily available.

Much of this development is good. It is wonderful to eat fruits that your own climate cannot possibly grow and national barriers are genuinely eroded by the exchange of foods.

But much has been lost. Supermarkets control food retailing and their demands are all about appearance and price. When you shop in a Mediterranean market you are expected to prod and poke, to handle food and smell it, even to taste it. Such behavior in a supermarket would bring the store detectives running. The quality of food is increasingly judged on its initial appearance, not on its taste or aroma. This is as absurd as the giant vegetables that dominate the amateur flower shows where we live, in the United Kingdom. A man (it is always a man) might be crowned champion onion/leek/ gooseberry grower without anyone ever tasting his onions, leeks or gooseberries. It is a kind of madness.

Most people are at ease with the concept of paying for the skills of a chef to convert raw ingredients into a complicated and delicious dish, but are less easy with the idea that the cook's role might be to do as little as possible in the process of preparing the food for the plate. To some extent it subverts the role of the cook and the ritual of dining out, where, so many might think, a performance is required and the more complicated and skillful it is, the better the value for money.

However, the quality and character of ingredients define the quality and character of the food we eat much more than the skill or ingenuity of their preparation.

At home (and arguably in a restaurant) we should not be trying to impress anyone with the skills displayed in cooking but simply in the tastiness of what we eat. Cooking at home is almost always constrained by time and the long, slow preparation of a meal, ideally shared with someone else, is the exception rather than the rule in every household. So the value of using ingredients at their best and absolutely freshest, which need the minimum of preparation, is practical as well as desirable.

The purpose of this book is to share our passion for providing ourselves with the freshest, tastiest ingredients to cook with, and to redress the role of food growing in the garden from the province of the male gardener who delivered a basket of produce to the kitchen door, keeping back what he considered to be the best (which invariably meant the biggest or straightest or roundest) for entering into the local flower show. It was very rare that the grower ever cooked his own produce.

To us this division makes both the gardening and the cooking incomplete and reduces the pleasure in eating. There was a time when everyone would have known exactly where their food came from and that intimacy was part of the ritual and pleasure of eating. As a society we have developed a depressing irresponsibility about what we eat. We recoil at the carcass of an animal lovingly tended and humanely slaughtered and yet ask no questions about factory-farmed, shrink-wrapped meat and dairy produce delivered to the supermarket shelf via conditions of appalling cruelty. We are so divorced from the practical production of what we greedily consume that we have stopped asking questions, as though ignorance was a justifiable excuse for factory farming, genetic engineering and the mass application of pesticides, insecticides and herbicides systematically applied to produce the gleaming rows of supermarket fruit and vegetables.

None of us is exempt from this. Modern life is too hemmed in and complicated to allow anyone to take too elevated a stance. But if you have a garden – however small – you can literally bring yourself back to earth and make those connections that are essential for sanity to prevail over what we eat. Growing fruit and vegetables is as important a part of the preparation of good food as anything you might do in the kitchen.

Traditionally, the kitchen and the kitchen garden have shared little other than name. The gardener (nearly always male) provided the raw materials and the cook (female) converted them into meals and neither intruded into the other's territory. We share the growing and cooking equally. There is no male/female demarcation line of what is proper for each gender to do and from the moment we choose the variety of seed we are thinking of it in terms of food on the plate.

No one in their right mind chooses to eat food that they do not like. We eat most of our meals at home and do not have access to a good local market with a supply of absolutely fresh fruit and vegetables. We like fresh food that really tastes of something and is not full of chemicals whose addition is for the convenience and financial advantage of grower, distributor and retailer but offers nothing to the consumer by way of taste or nutrition, which are the main reasons for eating the stuff in the first place.

Ingredients are the most important element in preparing food. We like simple, freshly made, uncomplicated food. Really good ingredients, eaten as fresh as possible, should always make a good meal, if not a delicious one. If you have a garden of any size you can make a significant contribution to the supply of fresh ingredients to eat at home. The important thing is that this is only a contribution. Self-sufficiency is for cranks. It is not an option for a varied and enjoyable diet. Everyone likes junk food to a greater or lesser degree. But we certainly don't want to live off junk food and it is important to have regular reminders of what good food is – which means having a regular source of fresh ingredients.

There is no attempt to grow anything that we do not enjoy eating. It seems completely reasonable and life-enhancing to only grow one crop of something that you love – to provide a few delicious meals a year and to leave it at that. Our own choice is unashamedly personal and eclectic. It is also strongly influenced by the history of the house and its geographical location. We do not struggle to produce stuff that will not flourish in its soil and microclimate. This is all part of reestablishing a connection to the natural world that carries on around you, whether you live in the center of a large city or on the remotest mountaintop. Nothing influences the food you can grow more than the weather, seasons and soil. Just growing a few herbs in a windowbox makes you aware of these things.

It also connects our entire diet. It is a wonderful thing to be able to eat avocados from Israel, lamb from New Zealand and beans from Kenya at the same meal, but completely removes any sense of locality or connection with place. It is better to savor food in season and go without it for most of the year than to eat an anodyne version of it weekly. Better to eat the best of local food – even if it is not perhaps as good as other food in other localities – than to reduce all meals to a domestic version of a takeout chain where the taste and ingredients are guaranteed to be identical across the world. Wherever you live there will be a tradition of producing certain ingredients and a tradition of certain ways of preparing them. This will be primarily influenced by the climate and geography of the place. It gives food meaning beyond mere sustenance.

This book is unashamedly about the way that we go about providing ourselves with fresh ingredients in our garden. It would be disingenuous to pretend that we do not spend much more time and energy – and even expertise – than most people would ever contemplate. We live in the country and have plenty of space. We are hardly typical. But we draw upon over 20 years of constant experience of growing food and cooking together. For 10 years we lived in the middle of London and did the same things on a much smaller scale. We have gardened and cooked when penniless, hiding out on the North Yorkshire moors, and grown food for large parties. We speak only from direct experience, but that experience spans quite a wide range of circumstances.

We lead very busy, complicated lives. We have three lovely, demanding children each with their own food fads and varying crazes. We do not have the time to spend hours every day cooking, even if we had the inclination. So most of the recipes in this book are simple, quick and with a very low demand on expertise. We can only reiterate our basic food philosophy, which is that the best ingredients, simply prepared, make the best food.

Monty and Sarah Don
Ivington, England

THE GARDEN

BY GROWING OUR OWN VEGETABLES it is like having our own private market permanently set up just outside the back door. But when we first came to this house in Ivington, England, in 1991 it was anything but a market. There was a small walled area in front of the house where vegetables had been grown for decades. The soil, we were assured by the old lady who had previously lived here for many years, was rich and productive. We had to take her word for it because by the time we arrived it was completely covered in building rubble left by the man we bought it from and was to remain so for the following 18 months.

The back of the house did not even hold the promise of good soil. The back door opened onto a small brick yard with a pigsty and well, and beyond that was a 2-acre field that was a tangled mat of grass, burdock and great pools of nettles, which we later worked out were the site of large elm trees that had been killed in the 1975–6 elm plague and under which cattle had sheltered.

This was the raw material we had to work with and that first summer of 1992 was spent cutting the grass, raking it all up and clearing the fallen tree trunks and stones that we uncovered as we cleared. In the spring of 1993 we plowed it all with a huge tractor and reversible plow. As the shining steel bit into the ground and turned it over we saw immediately that the soil was good. It was a rich clay loam over gravel, which is gardening gold. The natural tendency of the topsoil to retain moisture – and minerals – is moderated by the easy-draining subsoil. The site is only 150 feet from the river and is surrounded by water meadows that flood easily and often. The garden is on a raised plateau where, for centuries when the meadows flooded, the sheep and cattle must have been driven, manuring the ground. When the water gets really high – at least twice a year – a third of the garden is under water, so the drainage is vital. The area nearest the river contains hundreds of years of silt deposits and is a rich, crumbly black – quite different from the rest.

Because the house is set right in one corner of the site, which is a long rectangle, we could not relate the main lines of the garden to it. But starting from the house, you come out of the back door into the small backyard, through a gate into the small spring garden, which is dominated by the only tree that was here when we arrived, an old and exceptionally large hazel, kept I suspect for the nuts it invariably produces every September. It is underplanted with hellebores, early species roses, euphorbias, forget-me-nots, aquilegias, hostas and other shade-tolerant plants, narrowing down to a sliver before making a 90-degree left-hand turn to face the garden proper.

We made three long vistas going the full length of the garden, with a series of paths at right angles to these running along the width. In practice, this divides the garden into a grid, like an American city, and from above it is a series of seven interlocking blocks. As the blocks move away from the house, they become less manicured until the orchard—which, with its rough grass and overgrown boundary hedge, merges into the countryside.

THE VEGETABLE GARDEN

The main vegetable garden is the first of these blocks. It is roughly a square, measuring 66 x 69 feet. We planted hornbeam hedges around the outside, with interlaced limes rising above them. The idea is to make an enclosed place, protected from the wind but still light and sunny. As the site was completely exposed, we made woven hazel fences along the hedge lines to provide shelter until the hedges are established.

We decided that it should be divided into a number of small beds based around the two axes of crossing central paths. The beds were not to be raised in any conventional sense but were to have a low edging so that, as organic matter was added, the soil level could be allowed to rise above the paths. The principle behind raised beds is that they are completely accessible from the path so that you never have to stand on the soil. The beds are deeply dug initially and then organic material is added to the surface every year, removing – in theory – the need to dig again because the soil is never compacted. Our small beds do get stood upon occasionally and do get dug each year but, in theory at least, they are small enough not to be walked over and for the process of cultivation of each one not to be too daunting. This bit of garden comes in bite-sized chunks.

The division of the site into small, symmetrical beds not only provided visual structure, it also focused the cultivation onto very specific areas. It is important to make any aspect of your garden manageable within your own limitations but without compromising too much on your ambitions. Our 24 small beds mean that we can weed or dig one properly in half an hour and feel like we have finished a job; if we were cultivating only one twenty-fourth of a large plot, the result would be less encouraging.

The house is Tudor, so we borrowed from that period of gardening and wove low hazel fences around each of the beds. This involved weaving hundreds of hazel "rods", cut from local groves, around chestnut posts – which were cut from the only working sweet chestnut grove in Herefordshire. These posts are only 12 inches high above ground but have at least three times that amount below the soil and I found that they had to be banged in perfectly straight and in line if the weaving was to work. It was a great deal of labor. But the end product looked good and immediately imposed shape upon what was otherwise a plowed field.

The paths between the inner beds are only 18 inches wide and made of brick. But for the main paths and the 3 foot wide ring road we simply rototilled the ground and let it seed itself with grass. This works surprisingly well and quickly, especially if you cut off the weeds once a week to

The starkness of winter shows the layout of the vegetable beds with their woven hazel fences. These are not raised beds, and their layout is as decorative as it is practical, but they are small enough to limit the amount of compaction caused by walking on the cultivated soil and focus the cultivation onto productive areas.

stop them from seeding. Within three months the grass was dominant and within six it looked as though the paths had been there for years. But we should have taken more trouble, as one of our most pressing projects just five years later is to dig them all up and make them hard. If we had drained the ground properly – even if only with a layer of coarse sand – the paths would have been much more serviceable in winter. Also, grass paths at right angles to one another, edged by raised beds, are awkward to mow. Still, they were cheap and we had no money.

We saw an advertisement in the local paper for 70 mature boxwood plants that were "ready for collection" but, when we went to see them, found that what was for sale was an existing hedge. However, we dug them up there and then, and returned home with them packed around us in the car like green cotton wool, having paid a fraction of the normal retail price. They were then planted to form the lining down the main cross axis that leads to the flower borders, the wood garden and right down to the end of the orchard, so the view from one end runs the entire length of the garden and on out into open country – literally as far as the eye can see.

Boxwood has one great disadvantage in a vegetable garden in that it is a favorite hiding place for snails, which love the dry shade it provides. The roots also spread wide and have to be chopped back periodically, but this is not hard to do and the thick mat of roots adds a firm edging to the soil. Whatever its drawbacks, boxwood is indisputably the best structural plant for a vegetable garden, its green solidity the perfect foil for the exuberance of all vegetables from rhubarb to radishes.

Behind the boxwood hedge we planted a flanking avenue of espaliered pears, 'Williams' Bon Chrétien'. Actually, they started life intending to be pruned standards and were cut back and retrained as espaliers after a couple of years when they started to grow too vigorously. The espaliered branches are trained along a simple framework of canes lashed together. Unfortunately, these trees are cankerous; every year we cut back into uncankered wood and they grow back lustily but then get canker again. Sometime soon we will have to replace them.

We have an avenue of artichokes and cardoons (cousins of the artichoke) running down one side of the vegetable garden, bridging vegetable and flower garden. As the hedges and lime trees mature, this 10 foot wide strip will become too shady for them and they will have to be moved. As artichokes need to be replaced every two or three years to sustain a good harvest, this will not be a problem.

The central path takes you through the jewel garden borders (see page 203) into what we rather pretentiously call the wood garden or coppice. (We have always had trouble with the concept of naming different parts of the garden, unless they have an obvious function like the herb or vegetable garden. I know that some large gardens have separate areas with names alluding to other favorite gardens, towns or members of the family but that always seems rather strained.) It is planted with 70-odd hazels that we nurtured from self-seeded nuts from the original tree in the spring garden. There are oak and ash standards, all underplanted with bluebells, primroses, periwinkles and wild garlic. This is all fine and will be finer in years to come but as yet it is embryonic and looks pretty rough. Passing through the coppice, you arrive at the orchard.

THE ORCHARD

The orchard was planted in 1996 and 1997, so it is very young. Wherever possible we have used trees on vigorous MM111 rootstock, although some varieties were only available on MM106 rootstock, which is less vigorous, producing a half-standard tree. What we want to achieve is an orchard made up of large trees casting deep pools of shade in summer and with thick, lichen-covered branches in winter. Yes, standard trees are laborious to prune, awkward to collect fruit from and much slower to bear a decent crop than less vigorous forms such as a bush – but they are very beautiful, entirely typical of the area and who cares if they

are more work per apple? We are not running a business and it is naive to think you ever save money growing your own food on a small scale. Like every other edible part of the garden, the fruit fulfills our three criteria of tasting good, looking good and being chemically untreated.

This automatically discounts certain cultivars such as 'Cox's Orange Pippin', which is delicious but in our fairly wet position on the western side of England makes a scruffy tree, is very prone to canker and crops irregularly. Better to buy our 'Cox's' from a produce market and grow what thrives here, such as 'Ribston Pippin', from which 'Cox's Orange' was raised in 1825.

To set fruit the trees need to be pollinated (by insects) while in bloom. So, as no apples are reliably self-fertile (i.e. they will not pollinate themselves), another consideration when choosing trees for an orchard of any size is to include cultivars that will successfully pollinate each other. To do this you need to choose apples that are in flower at the same time, or that have at least an overlapping flowering period. Cultivars are allotted groups according to their flowering (and therefore fruiting) time, flowering group 1 being the earliest and group 7 the latest. The picture is slightly more complicated because some cultivars are incompatible and will not pollinate certain others even though they may flower at the same time, while some (known as triploids) are sterile and will not pollinate any other cultivars at all. Specialist fruit nurseries are the best source of advice when choosing which cultivars to grow.

Each tree was planted with great care, and involved preparing a hole 3 feet square. There is a case for not adding too much richness to the ground that fruit trees are planted in, but simply making sure that the ground is deeply dug and loosened to allow the roots a good run so that growth is not too sappy and vigorous at the expense of fruit. However, we want our trees to grow large and are prepared to wait for the fruit, so a generous amount of well-rotted manure was mixed into the subsoil before planting. The trees were also securely staked and tied.

I made the mistake in the first year of not removing apples as they matured. The result was that full-sized fruit bowed down the young, soft branches and when we had a storm in September a number of trees were damaged. It is important to be tough, removing most of the fruit from young apple trees until the branches are mature enough to bear the weight.

We planted the following dessert apple cultivars:

'Autumn Pearmain'	'Chivers Delight'
'Cornish Aromatic'	'Crimson Queening'
'Egremont Russet'	'Hambledon Deux Ans'
'James Grieve'	'Jupiter'
'King's Acre Pippin'	'Laxton's Fortune'
'Laxton's Superb'	'Madresfield Court'
'Mondial Gala'	'Orleans Reinette'
'Ribston Pippin'	'Rosemary Russet'
'Spartan'	'Stoke Edith Pippin'
'Strawberry Pippin'	'Tydeman's Early Worcester'
'Worcester Pearmain'	

We planted the following culinary apple cultivars:

'Arthur Turner'	'Blenheim Orange'
'Bramley's Seedling'	'Devonshire Buckland'
'Doctor Hare's'	'Glory of England'
'Grenadier'	'Herefordshire Beefing'
'Lane's Prince Albert'	'Newton Wonder'
'Norfolk Beefing'	'Peasgood Nonsuch'
'Rev. W. Wilks'	'Tillington Court'
'Tom Putt'	'William Crump'

The orchard also has an avenue of pears, made up of:

2 x 'Concorde'	2 x 'Conference'
2 x 'Doyenné du Comice'	2 x 'William's Bon Chrétien'

The pear trees are all grown on pear seedling rootstock, which will ensure very big trees. Like the apples, they would conventionally be described as "unmanageable", but what is there to manage? This part of the world is blessed with some of the oldest, and consequently biggest, pear trees to be seen anywhere; 50 foot pear tree in full blossom is one of the glories of the countryside.

Pears are planted just like apples, although they like more moisture so are better suited to heavier soil. The conventional advice is not to plant pears too deeply, in order to avoid scion rooting (the scion is the upper section of stem above the graft), which would encourage them to grow bigger at the expense of the fruit. So I deliberately planted ours deeper than advised.

The chickens have their henhouse in the orchard and scratch around the base of the trees, eating pests and adding to the general gaiety (except when they get into the vegetable garden, when my feelings toward them become murderous). Unfortunately, the price we pay for having free-range birds is a life expectancy of about 12 months before they are taken by foxes – often in broad daylight.

For all the talk of intended size and volume, the orchard hardly defines itself as a place yet, with the supporting stakes more dominant than most of the trees. This is especially so in winter but in summer the long grass and closely mown paths hint at what will be, although without the pools of shade that the trees will create. Of all the projects in the garden this is the most long term and requires the greatest faith; and yet, because of this, it is in many ways the most satisfying.

THE HERB GARDEN

The herb garden was made initially within the walled garden in front of the house and planted with old shrub roses among the herbs. But we found that the distance from the kitchen was inconvenient, especially in winter when we sometimes have to go out in the dark to collect the herbs. So we moved the herbs to the area that had formerly been part of the brick farmyard, just beyond the back door. This meant excavating 12 inches down into the stony ground and making raised beds, with retaining walls of oak boards 6 inches high to allow 18 inches of topsoil. We imported dozens of wheelbarrows of topsoil, and added lots of mushroom compost and sharp sand. Different herbs have different requirements but, knowing how shallow the soil was in these entirely artificial beds, our main concern was to provide good drainage.

The beds work very well and are very convenient for the kitchen. This underlies one of the major virtues of growing good ingredients at home, which is that, if carefully organized when it is laid out, the garden should be more convenient and "faster" than any store or fast-food service.

The herb garden is stocked for the kitchen and mainly limited to the perennial herbs that we use to cook with on a regular basis, namely rosemary, sage, marjoram, oregano, thyme, hyssop, fennel, lovage, bay, chives, tarragon, salad burnet, lemon balm and savory. Borage, chervil and dill are sown each year and basil, garlic and parsley grown on a larger scale in with the vegetables. Mint is grown in two old water troughs, and horseradish on a spare piece of ground, as both of these are too invasive to grow with other herbs.

The herbs are essential to the kitchen and we aim to provide ourselves with a limitless supply of the principal herbs so that we can cook generously with them rather than treating them as a precious garnish. This means restocking annually from seeds and cuttings.

ORGANIC GARDENING

We garden here organically. This means that we do not use pesticides or herbicides at all, that wherever there is a choice we buy organic seeds that have not been dressed with organophosphates and lindane, we use organically produced potting compost and, most importantly of all, recycle all "waste" so that it can go back into the system.

Organic gardening is not a system of rules to abide by or be punished for breaking. It is a way of looking at the world. The garden is a model of how we would like to live. We should all garden organically not because it is currently politically correct but simply because it is the most sensible and best way to make a good garden.

In the past it has been portrayed as a kind of branch of vegetarianism (which is ironic, as organic husbandry depends upon animals to provide manure and to graze) decorated with used yogurt containers and yards of black plastic. This was unsexy and dowdy and enough to turn anyone off. Gardens must be beautiful places in every regard or else they will not be used, and organic gardens are no exception to this.

The first thing to understand is that it is a holistic principle. A healthy garden depends upon all its working parts rather than just a few isolated components. Ideally, a garden should be self-sustaining or "non-input" as the Soil Association describes it. This goes against the current garden center culture of being able to buy anything for the garden. It means a slow and gradual establishment of an environment that largely provides for itself by supplying its own compost, weeding and recycling weeds, not adding very much fertilizer and not blitzing slug or aphid infestations but letting them settle into the restorative balance that any sudden imbalance will trigger. It is very like a healthily functioning body, where illness or hurt is inevitable but the body successfully heals itself, rather than throwing antibiotics at it and damaging the ability to self-heal in the process.

If you are trying to produce the tastiest, freshest food possible in your garden you must drop all the absurd competitive element that has dominated fruit and vegetable growing for the last century. Yet this attitude is still endorsed by the British gardening establishment from the Royal Horticultural Society down to local flower show committees. "Prize" anything is valued more highly than the environment and circumstances in which it was raised. This is an appalling aesthetic principle and at odds with all the wider pleasures of gardening, especially of growing food to eat.

molehills, sharp sand and sieved garden compost. But given that most people buy their seed-starting medium from a garden center, I would use a soil-based one, and then mix in the same volume again of perlite for seed sowing and cuttings, and half the volume for transplanting and potting.

• Perlite is expensive but essential. It keeps the medium open, making for good drainage and a free root-run and at the same time retaining moisture.

• Vermiculite is very good for seed sowing. I do not mix it into the medium but spread a layer on top of it to sow into, adding another layer to cover the seeds. It is the perfect consistency for the roots and top growth of seedlings to grow through and also stops any "capping" of the compost caused by watering and subsequent drying out, which can create a physical barrier to the emerging seedlings.

• Seeds sown indoors must be hardened off in their pots before planting out. The outside world is a cruel and shocking place after the safety of a greenhouse or windowsill. Put them out during the day for three or four days, bringing them in at night, then leave them outside for a similar period overnight as well, before planting them out.

• It is better to plant out indoor-grown vegetables when they are too small rather than too big, although you should not plant out anything less than two weeks after transplanting or potting – the roots need this length of time to grow into the new space. After that, watch them daily and as soon as you see roots appear through the bottom of the pot or you can take the rootball out of the pot without it falling apart, plant them out.

• It is no good lovingly tending a vegetable in the greenhouse, scrupulously preparing its various growing media, hardening it off slowly and then putting it into soil that is nothing like your medium. The ground must be properly prepared first, and some organic material, grit, and even perlite added to open it up, especially in the few inches immediately around the roots. On our clay loam, mushroom compost is unbeatable for this, rototilled or forked lightly into the topsoil just before planting out.

• If, when the plants are ready to be planted out, the ground is not free or the weather conditions are not suitable, any delay can be permanently damaging – you must pot the plants or else they will never properly grow beyond the potbound rootball. A slightly bigger pot with a bit of extra growing medium will give them a chance to grow unchecked until you can plant them out.

• Most seed trays are sold without the drainage holes properly drilled out. Good drainage is essential, so always check them and punch or drill out all the available drainage holes in the base before using them.

THE GREENHOUSES AND FRAMES

The greenhouse is essential to our garden. Almost all seeds propagate in there and develop as seedlings within its warm embrace. It is the one place that has constant growth at all times of year. Actually we have three greenhouses, although in many ways they are all different branches of the same essential "greenhouse" bit of the garden and the extra two have come about by accident rather than design. The main greenhouse is made of aluminium and entirely functional. Equipped with water and electricity for a mist propagating unit and heated benches as well as emergency electric heaters if the weather gets very cold, it is in a yard with the potting shed, cold frames and an area for hardening off plants. This is the boilerhouse of the garden. Its job is simply to be a plant factory, pumping out seedlings and cuttings, and in its industry lies its beauty.

The second greenhouse, 150 feet away in the soft fruit area off the orchard, was the propagating greenhouse until the new one usurped it and now it is used for early salad crops between January and May, which are then replaced by tomatoes with a few cucumbers and peppers. The tomatoes are underplanted with basil. Two-thirds of this greenhouse has beds that are planted directly into, and one-third is a separate section that we use for pots and grow bags. This greenhouse is also aluminium and is not heated at all.

The third greenhouse is a hybrid between a polytunnel and a greenhouse called a solar tunnel. It is made of reinforced polythene and has more tender crops like tomatoes, basil, cucumbers and peppers as well as seedbed and extra crops like chicory that do not like winter wetness. We also use it to overwinter tender plants.

It is a real luxury to have plenty of covered, protected space, which increases the range of crops and the period in which they can be grown. In the scheme of things they are not ruinously expensive, costing about the same as a good lawn mower or rototiller.

We also have homemade cold frames, which are used mainly for overwintering cuttings and tender plants and for hardening off seedlings raised in the propagating greenhouse. They then go from the cold frames to a sheltered strip along the length of the greenhouse before being planted out. The cold frames are not heated but lined 2 inch thick polystyrene and the glass is covered with sheets of bubble wrap to keep the temperature inside reasonably constant, which is the really important thing.

TOOLS

Our toolshed used to be the lower part of a hop kiln. The floor and walls are of brick and, because of the hop kiln, the ceiling is extraordinarily high. It is warm and cozy in winter and cool and dark in summer. The swallows swoop into the potting shed, around the corner, through the door into the toolshed and then nest in the rafters. Their seasonal return is all part of the rhythm and order of the tools, which hang in groups, spades on one wall, forks on another, hoes on another and odds and ends on another. We have a lot of hand tools because over the years I have not been able to resist buying them at sales or at local hardware stores in an unfamiliar town.

The truth is that I love garden tools. It does not matter what or where you are digging; a perfectly balanced, well-made spade with an ash handle makes it entirely pleasurable. There is an easy balance between hand and instrument when you use a good tool properly. So choose your tools with care, in the same way that you might choose a hat or a pair of walking shoes. They must feel right.

Any kind of planting is made easier by using good tools. Some time ago I took a pile of broken tools to be rehandled. Every time I went to collect them I was told that there was a delay: the guy was ill; the handle supplier was ill; the boss was on vacation. I seriously thought that I would never see them again. But finally a call came through to say that they were ready. It was worth every second of the wait. My pile of discarded and broken spades, forks, rakes, hoes and scythes had been fitted with lovely ash handles and the blades welded and adapted to fit, transforming them into a range of handsome, precise instruments.

Just to hold them makes me want to work with them. The deep pleasure of handling a tool that has been designed to perform a specific function as well as possible transmutes into the job itself. It is because tools are so specifically functional that they are beautiful – the artistry is in the artifacts. They have been refined over the centuries into the perfect form for a particular job. Most garden tools have reached a perfect stage of evolution and nothing shows this up so well as the occasional, laughable attempt to redesign a rake, spade, hoe or fork. It is like trying to redesign a shark or a thrush.

My favorite tool is a stainless-steel spade made in a foundry at nearby Wigan. I watched it being made through every stage from molten metal, right through the presses to the final sanding of the ash handle. That was 10 years ago and since then it has worked thousands of hours and is on its third handle. The blade is rounded and worn but good for another 20 years. No other spade has ever felt so apt in my hands. I use it for all planting, turf lifting and some weeding as well as digging.

We have quite a few other spades, accumulated over the years. There are smaller border spades, useful for working in the confined space of an herbaceous border, spades with foot treads and spades with long handles, an Irish garden spade with a narrow, very long blade and T-handle. Most of our spades and forks have YD-grips, made by cutting the ash handle and steaming it into a wishbone shape, which is then attached to the cross handle.

Garden forks are just as useful – and as used – as spades but never seem to have quite the same degree of character. You need a good, strong fork for digging and lifting heavy plants and another smaller one for weeding and more delicate work. We also have forks with finer and longer tines for turning compost, hay forks and flat-tined forks, called spading forks, which are used for breaking up hard soil.

A good hoe is vital. I once asked an old gardener the secret of his astonishing display of flowers: "I never lets that hoe rest," he said. I prefer Dutch hoes, which you push through the soil just beneath the surface, cutting the roots of weeds and leaving them on the soil to dry out or be raked up. We also have swan-necked hoes and draw hoes, which are used with a chopping action and are good for dealing with particularly tough weeds.

Since moving to Herefordshire I have learned to use what is called locally a stocker, which Americans call a Scovil hoe and I might have called a mattock. It looks like a draw hoe, but with no neck, and comes in various sizes, the biggest with a blade as large as a spade. I have found half a dozen at various farm sales and they are enormously useful for stocking: clearing very weedy and grassy ground before digging or rototilling. They are also ideal for earthing up.

Every garden must have a rake, and we use various types. There is a round-tined rake with straight steel tines that is best for preparing a seedbed. We have a heavy-duty, long-handled rake with aluminium tines, which is very useful for the stage between digging and raking – especially early in the year when the ground is still damp and lumpy. There is a rake that looks like a fork bent over at right angles with a very long handle, called a dung fork, originally designed for dragging manure from the back of dung carts, which we use exclusively for dragging and raking the soil after digging – it removes mounds and

breaks up the lumps extremely well. A wire rake is primarily for collecting leaves and scratching out moss on a lawn, but is also very useful on fine soil and for collecting longer grass. I love our wooden hay rakes, made locally entirely from ash, and used only to rake the long grass of the orchard twice a year. We have rubber rakes for raking up dead leaves and hoed weeds in the borders, because their rubber tines do not damage the growing plants.

I always carry a penknife in my pocket and my pruning shears live by the back door. If I go outside, they always come too. The best shears are made by Felco, and as I have always bought my shears without so much as a penny discount, I can say that without prejudice. I use a No. 8, which fits comfortably into my back pocket. Pruning is a job that should be done as and when you see it and you must have the tool at hand, which is why I like very light shears. I dislike anvil shears and never use them. Use the bypass type and keep them sharp and they will cut most things.

You need a good trowel and hand fork and stainless steel ones are best, although there are now nylon and plastic ones that are very light and seem to be strong. But nothing beats a good stainless-steel trowel for planting out.

Wheelbarrows are another area where technology has made improvements. We have always used metal builders' barrows, which are strong and cheap but last only about a year. Recently we have started using polythene wheelbarrows, which have proved to be very good indeed. Light, strong and durable – they are excellent. Buckets are essential. We use black builders' buckets for putting weeds in, dirty vegetables, compost, water, fertilizer, ash: anything that needs carrying.

There are all sorts of other bits and pieces that we use, some of them much treasured but nothing essential other than a portable radio, which has come to be invaluable. These may have been originally developed for Third World countries but ours has become a key component of the toolshed, where it lives, loaded into the wheelbarrow or carried every single time a job is done in the garden.

Whatever you grow, good hand tools are a joy. There is no objective judgment of what is "good" beyond performance, durability and ease of use. It is a very personal thing, and when you find something that is right the recognition is immediate and often grows, through usage, into a kind

 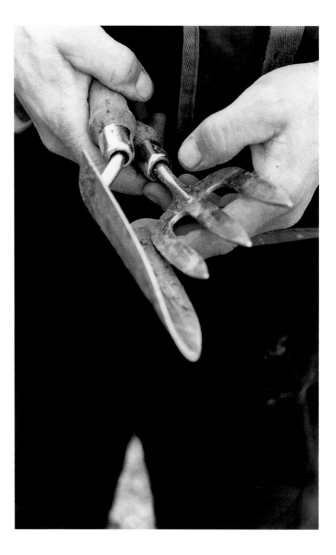

of love. This is a very practical relationship. Stainless steel makes digging tools much easier to use, especially on heavy soil. Provided they are treated with respect, tools, like my grandfather's scythe (opposite right), can give at least 50 years of pleasurable and invaluable use.

THE KITCHEN

SARAH'S FOOD PHILOSOPHY: I idealize a pure form of local food and a strong tradition of cooking rooted in the place. Herefordshire is rich in good food. One of the advantages of living here is the quality of the ingredients: Hereford cattle, local cheese, organic dairies, apples, pears, damsons, pear cider (perry), apple cider, game and free-range pigs for ham and bacon. Yet it has not always been so. In the past the food eaten on this farm was probably often bad. There are stories of rats gnawing through the cupboards, and of the weekly delivery of bread being eaten to the last crumb before the fresh bread was allowed to be touched – an attitude toward food as parsimonious as the minding of the last penny of the farm accounts.

I am always inspired by the way that Montagu is so generous and abundant with his harvests, bringing in wheelbarrows of fruit or armfuls of herbs from the garden rather than the litttle packages you get in the supermarket. There are times when I feel overwhelmed by the scale of the harvest. After two days spent making tomato sauce to freeze with the sun shining outside for the first time in weeks, opening a can seems more attractive. But I never regret it because this way I can make our own produce last most of the winter.

The food I cook is heavily influenced by the season. If I have a particular ingredient I cook it to eat fresh or to store, and if I don't have it I wait until its turn comes around. Our food is also strongly influenced by local conditions – we are landlocked and find it hard to get good seafood, and although there are fish in the river, salmon stocks are at the lowest level ever recorded.

I am inspired just by walking around the garden; whatever is at its best will usually be the basis of the next meal. A trip to the market or local town will also give me an idea of what to cook that day. I am all for going to market and buying good regional food in season – which is the accepted, if rather romanticized, view of food shopping in France and Italy. Yet I also rely guiltily on the vast, ugly local supermarket with its long opening hours and huge range of boring foods. I long to be a purist, but it would be sentimental and impractical. All too often, the shops in the surrounding towns with their early-closing days and screw-you attitude make shopping locally a depressing experience.

Good food is not easy to find. Everything has to be searched out, which takes time. But it is exciting to return home with fantastic ingredients to cook, like home-cured bacon from the market, a brace of pheasants and a bag of local apples.

The children have an important place here. They often cook for themselves, standing on a wooden chair, and we also cook for them several times every day. It is their kitchen as much as ours.

We normally sit down to lunch with whoever is around – and that is usually half a dozen adults, often more, plus double the number of children on weekends and holidays. The food we enjoy is home cooking, served collectively in large bowls for the entire table. It is food to be shared. I dislike hybrid food – it takes a very deft hand to combine exotic ingredients from all over the world and I can't do it. I am not a chef. I cook simply and I don't measure anything, rarely repeating a recipe exactly.

I have lived all over the world and my past is mapped out by memorable food. The scent of ratatouille cooking in Ramatuelle near St. Tropez when I was 14 was a revelation after a dreary diet of provincial English cooking. At 17 I ate

my way around Italy. I tasted pizza in Naples, pesto in Genoa – I can remember almost every meal I had there. Then, at 19, I was given a complete set of cookbooks by Elizabeth David, the Julia Child of English cooking. I had never cooked, but I knew how food should taste. To me the light and food of southern Europe lift the spirits in a way that northern Europe never can. I understand garlic, olive oil, brilliantly colored vegetables and Mediterranean herbs.

I envy the certainty of northern Italian and southern French cuisine. Although there are rumors about the disappearance of regional cuisines in Italy and France, the markets there are always an inspiration and still seem to serve the local population. In England we have long relied on imports such as spices, wine, oil and cane sugar to improve our food. As a family we grow much of our own food, but even we cannot live solely off the land; anchovies, olive oil and lemons are essentials in our kitchen.

Whenever I can, I buy organic food but it is not a religion or even a high moral stance. You cannot take a truly organic position without carefully researching the provenance of everything you eat. There is certainly no point in eating nasty food just because it is organic. We do not use any insecticides or pesticides in the garden and prefer to buy meat that is raised using traditional methods to maximize the taste of the resulting food. This usually means having to pay more, which is a choice that we are fortunate enough to be able to exercise. But buying processed food that is produced industrially is not always cheaper — there is a huge amount of packaging involved. Whenever we do a big supermarket shop the food all seems to go very fast without any of us having eaten noticeably more or better.

I hate the thought of eating vegetables sprayed with an invisible cocktail of fungicides and pesticides and enhanced with artificial fertilizers, combined with hormonally treated meat. I often wake in the night horrified by what the children have eaten: pigments in candy, let alone the unseen chemicals and the fashionable junk that they are tempted by. I know that organic food is costly and that if you are on a tight budget simply having enough food of any kind is the dominating factor. But growing some vegetables, herbs and fruit without the addition of weed killers and fertilizers does not have to be expensive and is safe to eat. The public horror over genetically modified food crops does not surprise me. How can anyone know what the long-term effect on our bodies can be? The realization that most of our food is irreversibly contaminated makes me feel helplessly alarmed. At least if we grow some of our own food we can control our diet.

In essence, my philosophy is that food should be a pleasure to grow and shop for, and that it should be easy and enjoyable to prepare as well as delicious to eat, at the very least doing you no long-term harm, and if possible doing you good.

THE KITCHEN LAYOUT

The kitchen was built in the 1570s as part of a timber-framed extension to the earlier medieval house. We know that there had been another building on the same site and it is very likely that the reused timbers were from this earlier building. The room is roughly 20 feet square with a very high ceiling. The floor is flagstoned and you can – and we often do – bring in wheelbarrows, muddy boots, bicycles and even, on one memorable occasion, a pony!

At least twice a year the river bursts its banks and floods up against the outer stone wall of the kitchen, the water sometimes 2 feet deep outside, although the inside remains bone dry. The swans swim up beneath the window when the river floods, but for most of the year cattle and sheep graze 6 feet away on the opposite side of the lane. The river flows 110 yards away across the field and we have watched otters playing on its banks. It is not a dramatic or grand

view, but is as agriculturally rural and unspoiled as is possible in the UK today.

We designed the kitchen ourselves, bought all the raw materials secondhand and had it fixed up on a very tight budget. There are only a few outlets (too few!) and everything is done as simply as possible. There is a large fireplace in one corner, with a derelict bread oven to one side, which is where the cooking would have been done originally and where the small Victorian range was set when we arrived. It now has a couple of armchairs and a sofa in front of it and the kitchen is as much a living room as a utilitarian food preparation area.

After the fireplace, the room is dominated by the 11 foot oak table. This was made for us by the carpenter who made and fitted all the doors and floors and who repaired the timber framing when we moved here. There was no design and not much discussion – he said that he would make us a table if we would like, and never mentioned it again until it was delivered (made to fit through the doors to a fraction of an inch). It is exceptionally beautiful and as treasured as any piece of furniture in the house. We use it for food preparation, eating, homework, drawing, reading the papers and, when it is very cold and the kitchen is the warmest place in the house, working on.

In the corner opposite the fireplace is the Aga, a stove common in England, bought in pieces from a builder's yard in Kington near the Welsh border. We had no idea if it worked or how to put it together but were assured by the builder that it came from "a very monied home." Who could resist such provenance? More to the point, we could not resist the price, which was less than a third of what a new one would have been.

The work surfaces are of thick slate that we bought from a farmer near Ledbury. They rest on brick piers, plastered and painted yellow like the rest of the kitchen. They are deliberately higher than most work surfaces to fit the proportions of the room, and for years the children complained that they could never reach anything – for a while Tommy kept a set of stepladders in the kitchen so that he could climb up onto them to get the candy that was supposedly out of his reach on a shelf.

There is a huge old Belfast sink – big enough to bath two children in when they were toddlers – which was here, unplumbed, when we came. The sink has a sycamore draining board (sycamore was always used for spoons and bowls, too, because it can take any amount of wetness and does not leave any taint on the food). Beneath the sink lives a large galvanized bucket for the vegetable scraps that are recycled to make garden compost. There are shelves for storage and a large corner cupboard containing food supplies, plates, glasses and cutlery.

Fixed to the great oak ceiling beams are rows of nineteenth-century hooks for hanging bacon, which was probably an important winter food here until at least the 1970s. We considered maintaining the tradition by keeping pigs ourselves, but they are notorious for escaping and the prospect of the damage they could do to the rest of the garden was enough to stop us.

The kitchen is not ideal and if we were to redesign it we would make it more practical, but it was done on a shoestring and has distinct character. It is a good place to be.

THE BACK KITCHEN

A door from the kitchen leads to the back kitchen, which contains a large brick bread oven, built at the beginning of the nineteenth century. The oven has a vaulted ceiling, walls at least 2 feet thick and its own chimney, and has worked perfectly from the first time we lit it. There is no reason to suppose that it has not been in constant use since it was built to replace the bread oven in the kitchen fireplace. In the back kitchen are also another large Belfast sink, draining boards, the washing machines and a dryer.

The floor is also of flagstones, which are washed down twice a week. All the coats and boots are kept here and any really dirty vegetables get washed in here before progressing to the kitchen. The muddy, wet dogs live here, too – resentfully, casting longing eyes at the rest of the house.

KITCHEN UTENSILS

I am resolutely anti-utensil, so there are fewer tools in the kitchen than in the garden shed. What I do have is practical, basic and uncomplicated, often bought secondhand or because it was all we could afford. When Tommy cooks he invariably uses everything before the operation is done.

I have mentioned the Aga and, apart from the bread oven, it is our only stove. I have a set of heavy stainless-steel, large Le Pentole pans, bought at what seemed vast expense in the mid-1980s but which have proved to be worth every penny and an extremely good value. I also have a large copper sauté pan, which is used often.

I use a set of Henkel knives, which are kept sharp. Knives seem a great luxury yet I am always on the lookout for more. Above the Aga is the normal range of spoons, ladles, whisks, sieves and forks, hanging from meat hooks on another bar; there is not really enough room for them and they are all crowded together. There are lots of wooden chopping boards but I still never seem to have enough. By the side of the Aga is a pot of wooden spoons and another of knives. Also by the stove are salt crystals, kept in a stoneware jar with a lid, and a pestle and mortar for grinding fresh pepper. There is a wooden box for the oils and vinegars, and the spices are above them on a shelf.

I have two big, square baskets full of baking pans and other equipment, all bought in a sale for about two dollars. Many of them – some of the pie molds, for example – are only used once in a blue moon but they are a luxury. There is a hand grater, which is used at least once every day.

We have a large catering fridge but only a small freezer, which is not really big enough. I use an ancient food processor and keep promising myself a new, big one. There is a pasta-making machine in a drawer, with all the parts, but it does not get used as much as it should. There is a treasured (by the children) toasted sandwich maker, which gets used far too much, and an equally chrome and gleaming cappuccino machine. Both are about as local and rural as a Soho bar.

SUPPLIES

Meat: If I cannot get certified organic meat – and it is very expensive and difficult to obtain – I make sure I know the origin of the meat. Do this by buying from a reputable butcher, or buy farm-killed meats. Always insist on free-range meat; that is the least you can do.

Free-range pork: Cuts of meat, sausages, bacon and ham.

Welsh lamb: When we have eaten up our own lambs, I buy Welsh lamb. The lambs are grass fed and as free ranging as you can get.

Game: Pheasants and pigeons are a good source of wild meat. I buy them plucked, trussed and dressed as a brace, a cock and hen side by side. Venison, mainly roe, is culled from the local woods. Farmed venison is widely available.

Poultry: I get fresh chickens, ducks and geese from local farms, or specialist poultry dealers.

Fish: I buy fish from the market in Hereford, or a wholesaler in Ludlow who will get pike from local fishermen.

Fresh produce: Free-range eggs (from our own hens), or the freshest organic eggs if our own hens are not laying.

Cheese: There are many small, independent cheese-makers, and I much prefer to use these rather than buy industrially produced cheeses even if they are not always organic.

Mushrooms: Field mushrooms in season, depending on the year's weather conditions, or I buy organic chestnut mushrooms.

Gingerroot

Lemons and oranges: I buy organic, unwaxed fruit whenever possible. Scrub them before you use them anyway.

Raw honey: Local honey is best – you supposedly never get hay fever if you eat enough of your local honey.

Apple cider and Pear cider: Westons prize winning strong organic cider is delicious and tastes just like the cider of my childhood. Cider brandy is distilled in Hereford, and is equal to Normandy calvados. Perry pears are getting rarer, but perry is worth seeking out – either dry and still, or you can get a fizzy version.

THE PANTRY

Salt: Sea salt is composed of naturally formed crystal salt flakes, and is not too strong. We crumble it over food.

Black pepper: Always grind the pepper freshly each time you use it. A pestle and mortar is best for this.

Olive oil: Use organic olive oil. If you are frying or heating it up to boiling point, don't bother using extra-virgin olive oil – save that for dressings.

Extra-virgin olive oil: This is worth the expense because it is so delicious and much healthier than butter.

Unsalted butter: Always get this from an organic source. I use it mainly for cooking – pastry, stuffings and so on – but it is also good with bread and jam.

Salted farm butter: This salty butter is perfect spread on Montagu's freshly made bread, and I also use it for making herb butters.

Organic cane sugar: Either granulated or caster sugar. Even powered sugar comes in a golden unrefined form.

Flour: Organic strong white bread flour. We buy this by the 70 pound sack. Although you are not really supposed to use it for cakes, I use it for all our baking, including pizza and pasta.

Pasta: A very good organic dried pasta is available now.

Risotto rice: Arborio rice is the one most widely available.

Dried fruits: Organic raisins, yellow raisins, apricots.

Vinegars: For making chutneys I use wine vinegar or cider vinegar, and also have balsamic vinegar for salad dressings.

Dried chili flakes: If we run out of fresh chilies.

Anchovies: Salted or packed in oil.

Vegetable stock: If you don't have the time or inclination to make stock, Knorr is acceptable but very salty. Use it very sparingly.

Nuts: I use our own hazelnuts when they are fresh. Pine nuts are used for pesto, but I also use walnuts for a winter pesto made with parsley.

Spices: Whole nutmeg, to be freshly grated as needed, star anise, juniper berries, vanilla pods, cinnamon sticks, whole cloves, cayenne pepper, mustard seed.

SEPTEMBER

SEPTEMBER ALWAYS COMES to this part of the world as a reward. In a way, it is where the gardening year arrives. It is the month of harvest but the start of the next year's cultivation and planning as well, and this paradox of old and new is juggled within the kitchen garden with beans, onions, sweet corn, self-blanching celery, chard, the last of the summer lettuces, squashes, tomatoes and basil all needing to be collected before the end of the month if they are not to be wasted. No other month has such a rich and rounded light or such a tangible sense of preciousness. But, of course, with that arrival is a real sense of loss because everything from now until Christmas is downhill.

I see that in my garden diary for 1998 I wrote on September 11, after we had been away for a week: "Went away in summer and came back to autumn."

Certainly, over the course of just a couple of days the season seems to shift and, after all the bustle and control of the previous three or four months, there is nothing that one can do about it. Every day the light is slipping away and there is not a moment of it to waste.

Also slipping away are the swallows, massing by the score over the garden to fatten up with insects before, suddenly one morning, we notice that they have all left on their 4,000 mile journey to Africa. It is the truest signal that summer is over.

This is not a hardship. Decline can be beautiful and, after all, right across the Northern Hemisphere, this is harvesttime. Our garden is surrounded by fields and the evocatively dry, strawy smell of newly cut corn is an intrinsic part of our garden in September.

So, despite the sense of the year being on the wane, the garden is filled with vegetables and fruits and has a rich sense of repleteness. What this means to the kitchen is that we are bringing in either too much or too little of everything. September inevitably is a time when the steady supply of lettuces, radishes, beans and peas diminishes and there is concurrently a lot of surplus of other crops such as tomatoes, basil and onions. September is the month of chutneys, jams, soups and sauces for freezing. There is also a subtle shift of emphasis in the vegetable garden. As the summer crops are harvested and cleared, the winter crops such as the various cabbages, leeks, cardoons and chicories step forward and take center stage.

The tomatoes are reddening daily, racing ripeness against the light. The 'Gardener's Delight' hang in herringbone trusses of plum-sized fruit colored from green to orange to bright red like crazy traffic lights. They are not a glamorous variety but easy to grow, reliable and – above all – tasty.

Along with the harvest there is much to be sown, both for an autumn crop and to overwinter for next spring. At the beginning of the month we sow lettuce, chicory, endive, mizuna, rocket, corn salad, winter purslane and chervil. The thinnings can be eaten in October, with the main plants surviving the winter before growing in early spring when salad crops are few and far between. The ground that the French beans have grown in is ideal for these autumn crops, as their roots have opened up the soil and "fixed" nitrogen for the leaf crops to use. I pull up the plants, quite happy to leave plenty of root behind as it will all add to the soil structure, then fork over the ground and rake it immediately, having the seeds in the ground within minutes of clearing it so that they have as much chance as possible to germinate and grow.

Because the soil is warm and the nights cool, there is always a dew, so there is moisture, and the ground is neither too warm nor too cold. So germination and initial seedling growth is very fast.

One of the jobs that best belongs to September is the taking of boxwood cuttings. Boxwood is traditionally used for edging in kitchen gardens and nothing else gives such a good and constant structure around the rambling growth of vegetables.

Cuttings are very easy to take and give you a supply of plants for practically no expense. Time is the factor that you pay for because boxwood grows slowly and a cutting taken in September will not make a hedging plant for two years. But in three or four years' time it will be growing strongly. If you get into the habit of taking some cuttings every September, you soon build up a stock of plants.

Choose strong-growing shoots about 6 inches long, cutting back just into last year's wood. This is not essential but the old wood acts as a plug, delaying drying out of the stem before roots can form. Strip off the bottom 3–4 inches of leaves and push the stem 2 inches deep into a growing medium made up from a mixture of half ordinary potting soil and half perlite. I use 3 inch square pots, putting in five cuttings to a pot. Water lightly and put into a cold frame, if you have it, or underneath the bench of a greenhouse. The idea is to keep them moist but not wet, to protect them from hot sun but to provide some light. Leave them until well into next spring. Roots should have formed by then. Take them out of the pot and either pot them up individually or line them out in the vegetable garden before planting out the following spring.

It is a slow business, but very easy and curiously satisfying. They do, by the way, take pretty well put into open ground that has sharp sand or grit added to it, and topped with a row cover.

BASIL

Just as basil combines perfectly with tomato in the mouth, so do they make ideal companions in the garden. Plant basil, both outdoors and in the greenhouse, at the base of tomatoes, where they will share the same desire for strong sun, rich soil and plenty of water. If you grow basil in the

A wheelbarrow of basil rushed straight from garden to kitchen. Basil is easy to grow from seed, and one packet will provide basketfuls of leaves that can be used throughout the summer. Grown in a sunny spot outside, basil is tough and vigorous, although it will not survive any frost, so we lift all the plants in September for making into pesto and freezing. The quicker it is frozen, the fresher it tastes when thawed.

herb garden there is a real risk of underwatering it or of overwatering neighboring Mediterranean herbs that relish any amount of heat and drought that our northern summers can throw at them.

If you live in a temperate zone, the period between the end of summer and the beginning of autumn is always fraught with tough decisions about timing the harvest. On the one hand you want to maximize the available good weather to encourage as much growth and ripening as possible, while on the other you risk losing everything with an early frost.

Most herbs will survive our winter even though they do not produce any new, tender growth and the existing top growth will variously die back (as with mint), wither (thyme) or slowly fade until replaced by vigorous new growth (sage). Their "harvest" diminishes until, by about Christmas, there is nothing there and we have to wait until March and April.

Basil is, however, an exception. Frost kills any trace of it and usually arrives just as the basil is at its most prolific. Throughout the summer we use it here and there, in salads and in cooked dishes (where, unlike most herbs, it increases in taste as it cooks – the strength of the taste of basil in the dish should therefore be regulated by when it is added). But on the whole, supply far exceeds daily demand.

Then comes the moment of crisis, around the middle of September for us, when we can risk it no longer and have a huge pile of basil from hundreds of plants to deal with. It cannot be frozen, and drying loses much of its flavor. Luckily, there is a synergy between the glut of basil and the demand for frozen pesto. Although basil leaves will not successfully freeze, when mixed up with oil, garlic and pine nuts to make pesto (leaving the Parmesan until after defrosting) it freezes well and thaws out as fresh as the day it was made. Thus, one has the perfect balance between garden and kitchen.

It takes large amounts of basil to make generous helpings of pesto for five of us – hence the hundreds of basil plants. The secret is to make the pesto as soon as possible after harvest. We have enough leaves to fill a wheelbarrow, which is wheeled right into the kitchen before the contents are lifted in great armfuls onto the table and turned into pesto right away. This haste matters because it makes all the difference to the freshness of the taste of the pesto.

We sow the basil seeds in seed trays in April. As soon as they are large enough to handle, they are transplanted into individual pots and left to grow on in the greenhouse until June. Basil is delicate and prone to damping off (getting a fungal infection that causes little seedlings to wilt and die) but needs plenty of water as it grows. We harden the plants off by putting the trays of plants outside the greenhouse for a couple of weeks before planting them out in full sun, with plenty of manure or compost in the ground, as they really respond well to rich soil. Water them regularly and never let them dry out or else they grow woody and the leaves get leathery. It is best to pinch off the flowers as they appear, as they coarsen the leaves.

Purple basil, *Origanum basilicum* 'Purpurascens', looks wonderful and is good raw in salads, but is not nearly so good for pesto as its green sibling. Bush, or Greek, basil (*O. basilicum* var. *minimum*) is a native of South America, and makes a compact bush with tiny leaves that is hardier and good for general cooking but not really suitable for pesto.

FLORENCE FENNEL

Florence fennel is a crop that is tricky to get fully mature before summer runs out. It has a tendency to bolt and go to seed before the base swells sufficiently. I think that the secret is to sow the seeds late and to encourage them to grow as fast as possible with plenty of water and goodness in the soil. Two or three sowings spaced across a month or more will give the best supply. In a warm year it is better to sow the seed directly outside, making the first sowings at the end of May and thinning the seedlings to 9 inch spacings. This has the great advantage of not disturbing the roots – which grow very large – but Florence fennel is very susceptible to slug attack at the seedling stage. In a cold year it is better to sow the seeds in a seed tray in May, transplanting them into individual pots as soon as they are large enough to handle. Grow them for a month under cover, harden them off for a few days outside and then transplant into blocks at 9 inch spacings. Keep them well watered and weeded and earth them up as the bulbs begin to swell.

Even if the bulbs fail to grow very big, the whole plant is delicious chopped up and cooked with roast pork, which absorbs all the flavor of the vegetable.

Toward the end of summer it always becomes a race against time to see if certain crops will mature before the cold weather stops them. I suppose our climate is too cold for them really, but for some, like sweet corn, Florence fennel, and squashes and pumpkins, it is worth seeing if you can produce a decent harvest in the period between late May and early September when frost is very unlikely.

SWEET CORN

Sweet corn is one of those crops, like asparagus, new potatoes and peas, which tastes at its best within minutes of harvest. Any delay between picking and eating reduces the quality of the culinary experience. The water should be boiling before the cob is picked and then it should be boiled and eaten with butter without any distraction.

In principle, sweet corn is easy to grow as long as the soil is well manured and the site sunny. It is best sown indoors in April in individual pots or units, putting two seeds in each pot. The temperature must not fall below 50°F if the seeds are to germinate, but once they have, remove the weaker of the two seeds. Grow them in the greenhouse until the end of May before hardening off outside for a week. Plant out in a grid at 18 inch spacings. A grid, as opposed to a single line, is necessary for good pollination of the plants. Water well, especially after flowering, and keep weeded.

The cobs are ready to be picked when pressing an individual grain produces a creamy liquid. Pick it by twisting off the whole cob from the stem and then rush to boiling water!

FRIDAY, SEPTEMBER 25:
Dry. Cloudy. Drizzly PM.
Sarah picked 55 lbs tomatoes. Still much more again left (all in top greenhouse).
I took a dozen cuttings from rosemary with virus – will they inherit it?

TOMATOES

Although the tomatoes in the greenhouse are left well into October, I find that it is not worth leaving outdoor tomatoes to go on ripening past the end of the month. We pick the ripe or ripening fruits and pull up the whole plants with green tomatoes attached. These are then hung upside down in the potting shed and the fruits continue to ripen.

Whatever the variety, tomatoes must be sown under protected conditions, like a greenhouse, cold frame or windowsill. Unless they are to be grown with controlled heat, there is no virtue in sowing too early. I find that the first two weeks in April is early enough.

Sow thinly in seed trays. They will take about 10–14 days to germinate. As soon as two true leaves form – about 14 days after germination – they should be transplanted into individual pots or cells. Keep them in a greenhouse in full sun and do not let them dry out. Water with a commercial liquid feed twice a week. Let them grow for about four weeks before planting out in the greenhouse in May or a sunny position in the garden in June about 24 inches apart. Plant them slightly deeper than their position in the pot, as they will grow roots from the stem, which helps to support them as they grow. We grow 'Shirley', 'Alicante', 'Gardener's Delight' and 'Marmande'.

Tomatoes conventionally have better flavor when grown outside, but they must have a very sunny position with good ventilation. Indoors or out, they will need rich, well-drained soil, although they grow perfectly satisfactorily in grow bags or pots. The advantage of a pot versus a grow bag is that the former will take a cane, which is really important as the plants mature, as they will need support

This will stop the tomatoes from becoming watery and tasteless when ripe. As the fruits begin to swell, remove the leaves below the first fruits and thin others to improve ventilation. Repeat this process toward the end of summer. In my experience you can be fairly radical about this thinning process without harming the plants, and it improves both air circulation and the ripening of fruit.

Fruits are ready to pick if they come away in the hand when gently twisted. If they start to split, this is a sign that they need more water. Pick the splitting fruits and water each plant well. By the beginning of October any remaining fruits will ripen best indoors in a warm room or a drawer. Green fruits can be made into chutney, which is delicious.

HAZELS

Outside our back door we have a single, large hazel tree. This was the only tree or bush growing in the area behind the house – which comprises by far the majority of the garden – when we came to Ivington. In our first September we discovered that it produced a huge crop of hazel nuts and has done so every early autumn since.

Growing nuts for deliberate harvest is rare in modern gardens, but until the twentieth century they were a much-valued crop. A nuttery is a kind of nutty orchard and a lovely notion, with its own botany of plants adapted to the cycle of coppicing. Over the past five years we have collected the young hazel plants that have germinated from nuts buried by squirrels and planted 70 or so of them to make our own nuttery. It is slow to get going but in five years' time should come into its own. Hazels will grow almost anywhere although a hazel coppice will produce straighter, stronger stems for coppicing on wet, rich soil but tends to produce better nuts on stony, poor soil. The nuts are not the fruit but the seeds of the tree. These are rich in oil so have a high nutritional and caloric value and are deliciously sweet as well.

The wild hazel of woodland is *Corylus avellana*, or the cob. It was given the name of St. Philibert, a seventh-century

from the first few weeks after planting out. The cane needs to be strong enough to support a 6 foot high plant loaded with a heavy crop of fruit.

Keep them well watered as the plants develop, feeding once or twice a week. As the plants grow they develop three types of lateral growth: stems just bearing leaves, branches with fruit (known as trusses); and strong stems in the axes between the stalk and the horizontal leaf stems. The latter should be pinched out as they develop, as they use a lot of the plant's energy that would otherwise go into producing fruit.

Ease off the water once the fruits start to grow, cutting back to once a week outside and every few days indoors.

Benedictine. This has become filbert. Confusingly, we now classify *C. maxima* as a filbert and differentiate it from a cob by the way that the husk completely envelops the nut, which, in turn, is rather longer than the more rounded cob.

The nuts should be allowed to ripen on the tree and gathered as soon as they fall, and will store until Christmas if kept in their husk, which stops them from drying out too fast. If collected while still green, leave them in a dry place and they will ripen by about November.

PLUMS AND DAMSONS

There were a few scrawny plum trees when we moved in here and they do produce fruit, but they are temperamental. Sometimes they half ripen on the tree and are eaten by the wasps before we can pick them and at other times they linger unripe – until you go away for a weekend and they all ripen at once and fall to the ground. I have planted one tree of 'Oulin's Gage' and two of 'Old English Greengage', but it will take a few years before these provide any kind of harvest. They are all grafted onto 'St. Julien A' rootstock. which makes a fairly vigorous tree but which can also be fan- or herringbone-trained against a wall. Plums like a rich soil and a sunny site (although 'Czar' will ripen on a shady wall), so are planted with plenty of manure added to the planting hole and the surface mulched annually with compost. Like all standard fruit trees, they must be staked and tied securely for at least the first five years.

Plums tend to do well in this western side of England because of our high rainfall and relatively mild climate but, in this localized borderland between England and Wales, damsons – that astringently sweet plum bought back by the Crusaders in the twelfth century – are the prize fruit of September. Damsons are compact, tough, easy to grow, largely self-fertile and come true from seed. They have been ignored by plant breeders, so a variety such as 'Shropshire Damson', which would almost certainly have grown 500 years ago in the orchard of this Tudor house, will taste now exactly as it did then, spanning the gastronomic centuries.

There are damsons growing in our hedgerows that provide fruit as cultured as anything pampered in an orchard, but I have also planted a single 'Farleigh Prolific' to boost supplies for the future.

Damsons were not just eaten but also used in the glove industry, which was an important local industry here during the eighteenth and nineteenth centuries. The juice was used as a dye and anyone who has gotten damson juice on their hands and clothes will know how effective a stain it is.

Although these small, oblong plums can be eaten uncooked, damsons are usually cooked in various ways so that they can be stored. No other fruit has so intense a flavor, and in midwinter the sharp, fruity tang of damson draws you straight back to early September. Traditionally, damsons were baked in pies and stewed to be eaten fresh, and made into jams, "cheese" and chutneys for storing. They are one of the few fruits better preserved in a mason jar than frozen, and the rich, red fruits swimming in crimson liquor are an ornament on the shelf. We also make damson sorbet.

Damson cheese is one of those eighteenth-century recipes that fits in perfectly with modern life. When cider apples are crushed and formed into a layered block, the resulting pomace that the juice is pressed from is still known as a cheese, and my guess is that damson cheese is so called because the boiled fruits are placed in a muslin bag and the juice drips from this, leaving a dry(ish) "cheese" like the cider apples. This intense, rich juice sets to make a very stiff, opaque jelly that is the best accompaniment for game, lamb (what my youngest son calls lamb jam), cold meats, pies or strong cheese. It will keep in a cupboard for years.

PEARS

Pears flower earlier than apples and pear blossoms are one of the first – and best – indicators of spring. But they are consequently more prone to damage by late frosts, so always plant in a protected site, sheltered from cold winds. They do better on wet soil than apples but grow best on well-drained, fertile ground. The one thing they do not like is drought, so mulch them well each year and water in dry weather. This can be especially important if they are planted against a south wall, which is always very dry. Pears are usually grown on quince rootstock – unless especially large trees are required, in which case they are grown on pear seedling rootstock. 'Quince A' is more vigorous than 'Quince C' and is best for standards, tall espaliers or anything less than very good soil.

Like apples, pears need a pollinating partner – although 'Conference' is partially self-pollinating it is more reliable if it, too, has another variety to pollinate with. There are four flowering groups of pears. Wherever possible, choose two or more varieties from the same group, although adjacent groups will usually pollinate. Where you are growing long stretches of espaliered pears, intermingle the groups regularly to increase pollination. When a pear is triploid, such as 'Jargonelle', 'Merton Pride' or 'Catillac', you need three varieties to make the fruit: a pollinator and a third nontriploid variety to pollinate the pollinator.

If that all sounds daunting, the following well-known and easily available cultivars from flowering groups 3 and 4 all pollinate successfully within their group:

Group 3

'Beurré Hardy'	'Concorde'
'Conference'	'Williams' Bon Chrétien'

Group 4

'Beth'	'Doyenné du Comice'

Pears fruit from spurs two or more years old, therefore pruning is geared at building a framework of branches carrying plenty of these short, fruiting spurs. In July the growing tips are cut back by half to strong buds, leaving the framework to be tied in as required – be it as espaliers, cordons, bushes or trees. In winter these spurs can be pruned back again to three or four buds and any crossing or damaged branches pruned right back. It is good practice to mulch after pruning.

ROAST PORK MARINATED WITH FENNEL AND PEAR CIDER

This is cooked with two types of fennel – the fresh bulbs of Florence fennel and dried seeds of the herb. The first time I made this I used some young fennel bulbs that Montagu had brought in from thinning out in the garden. Fennel is one of my favorite herbs and we harvest enormous quantities of the seeds each year. Cooked like this, the pork will be meltingly soft and rich, and permeated with the aniseedy flavor of the fennel. It seems to make the pork more digestible.

Perry is a cider made with a hard little pear that grows in Herefordshire and the West Country. If you can't get hold of it then a dry real cider will do, as long as it is not an industrial cider made with apple concentrate.

If you buy the roast with crackling, prepare in the same way, but be careful not to burn it in the initial stages of cooking. The crackling should be crisp, not greasy or rubbery, and it is important to salt it well to draw the moisture out.

Any large boned pork roast, e.g. shoulder, leg or loin, about 4 lbs
Sea salt
2 tablespoons fennel seeds
2 tablespoons olive oil
2 cups pear cider (or dry cider)
4 fennel bulbs
Serves 8–10
Oven temperature: (to start) 450°F (then) 300°F

Score the skin of the roast and rub in crushed sea salt, the fennel seeds, oil and half the perry. Cover and leave to marinate in a cool place for up to 24 hours.

Slice the fennel bulbs and lay them over the bottom of a large roasting pan. Place the marinated roast on top, with its

juices and the rest of the perry poured over. Roast in the preheated hot oven for about 30 minutes, checking to make sure the pork is not burning. Then reduce the oven temperature to low and continue roasting for about $2\frac{1}{2}$ hours, basting the meat with the juices in the pan every 20 minutes or so.

Take out the pork and keep warm on a carving dish. Remove the sliced fennel with a slotted spoon and put in a serving dish. Keep warm.

Pour off the roasting juices from the pan, and separate and discard the fat. Boil up the juices again, check them for seasoning and consistency – they may need thinning down a little – and serve as a sauce with the meat.

PESTO

When I was 17 I first ate pesto on the docks of Genoa, and I thought it was the most delicious, aromatic thing I had ever tasted. It was served simply on thin spaghetti. I have tried to re-create the taste of it ever since.

I make it in batches, since there is so much basil to process. I love the sight of the kitchen table covered in a mountain of plants that have been cut off at the base. Everyone helps strip the leaves off and the room is scented with the pungent scent of basil, which can be overpowering in that quantity. Our children would eat this every day given a chance, so it doesn't last long. If it is to be frozen, make it without the cheese, then add this later when thawed.

6 oz fresh basil leaves, picked and separated from stalks

2 oz pine nuts

3 cloves mild fresh garlic

$\frac{1}{2}$ teaspoon coarse sea salt

$\frac{2}{3}$ cup olive oil

3 $\frac{1}{2}$ oz Parmesan cheese, freshly grated

1 oz pecorino cheese, freshly grated

Serves 12

Combine the basil leaves, pine nuts, garlic and salt in a food processor, or crush together with a pestle and mortar. If making in a machine, add the olive oil through the feed tube as a steady stream and process for a few seconds; if making by hand, slowly incorporate the oil into the mixture. If it is going to be eaten quickly, add the cheese now. If not, put the pesto into little containers and freeze it.

As you mix the sauce with the pasta and warm it all together, you can thin it down with more oil.

ROASTED TOMATO SAUCE

I have tried lots of methods for tomato sauce, and this is the best one for getting maximum flavor from rather watery tomatoes. To store this, I divide the sauce into quarters (each is enough for a meal) and put it into little containers.

5 lbs fresh tomatoes

4 cloves garlic, sliced

Sea salt

Sugar

Olive oil

Serves 24

Oven temperature: 450°F

Cut the tomatoes in half, and place cut side down in a large, deep roasting pan. Sprinkle with the garlic, sea salt and a little sugar, and drizzle with olive oil. Roast in the preheated oven for 40–60 minutes. A lot of water will bubble out of the tomatoes, and the idea is to reduce this by evaporation until you get a concentrated flavor.

This is beautiful as a vegetable dish in its own right; it could be served just as it is with a little more fresh garlic and fresh basil leaves (or thyme or oregano would be just as nice) tucked in just before serving.

To make into a sauce, scrape off every little bit out of the pan, and whir it in a food processor. It will keep for at least a week in the fridge with a little olive oil floated on top, or can be frozen for the winter and used for pasta sauces, soups and pizza.

FRESH TOMATO SAUCE

Because we always have a glut of tomatoes, I usually make this sauce in large quantities and freeze it for use throughout the winter.

2 lbs fresh tomatoes

4 tablespoons olive oil

Bunch of fresh thyme

Pinch of sugar

Sea salt

Pat of butter

Serves 6

Skin the tomatoes, first dipping them in boiling water for a few seconds to loosen the skins. Either process briefly in a food processor, or chop roughly. Simmer the tomatoes in a sauté pan with the olive oil, bunch of thyme, sugar and a pinch of salt for about 30 minutes or until reduced by half, stirring from time to time. Taste for seasoning, remove the herbs and add the butter. This sauce will be a pale vermilion color, with a fresh taste.

TOMATO CHUTNEY

When there is a glut in each season we simply make chutney. This keeps us going until Christmas, and it is very good with bread and cheese or cold meat. If the tomatoes have been blighted and there are lots of unripe tomatoes, this works just as well with green or red tomatoes.

2 $\frac{1}{4}$ lbs cooking apples

4 $\frac{1}{2}$ lbs tomatoes, chopped

3 medium-sized onions, chopped

1oz gingerroot, peeled and grated

1 lb 10 oz sugar

4 tablespoons yellow raisins

3 $\frac{1}{2}$ cups cider or white wine vinegar

1 tablespoon sea salt

1 heaping teaspoon cayenne pepper

Makes about eight 1 lb jars

Peel, core and roughly chop the apples. Soften the apples in a large heavy-bottomed pan in a little water. Add all the remaining ingredients to the apples, and bring gently to a boil. Simmer for about 1 hour, until thickened.

Allow to cool slightly, then fill sterilized jam jars that have been warmed in the oven so that the glass doesn't crack. Seal with jam pot covers (a waxed paper circle and cellophane cap).

DAMSON CHEESE

Damson cheese reminds me of ancient sweetmeats, which you still see in the spice market of Istanbul. It is the perfect foil for venison as well as lamb or the Christmas goose, with its blackish purple color and rich flavor. It is a thick opaque jelly, not really a cheese at all. It is useful to add sweetness to sauces and gravies.

6 lbs damsons

4 cups water

6 lbs sugar, warmed in a low oven

Makes at least a dozen 1 lb jars

Simmer the whole damsons in the water until soft and the pits rise to the surface. Press through a nylon sieve, using a wooden spoon, and return the pulp to the pan. Add 1 lb of sugar to each 1 lb of pulp. If you have the inclination, crack some of the pits and add the kernels to the sieved fruit to add a slight bitterness to the cheese. Boil until it reaches the setting point, stirring constantly to prevent it from burning on the bottom. To test for setting, put a drop onto a cold saucer; leave to cool, then push the side of the drop with your finger to see if it wrinkles. If still runny it needs to boil for longer. It will be a thick, fudgy mixture, more grainy than a jelly. Pour into sterilized, warmed jam jars and cover with waxed discs and cellophane covers.

PLUM AND HAZELNUT TART

When we first moved into this garden, the only edible things growing were a plum tree and a spreading hazel. The nuts from the latter arrive in late summer by the hundred and are delicious, although the squirrels take half of them. The plum tree is equally prolific.

For the pastry

6 oz unbleached plain flour

2 oz caster or granulated sugar

Pinch of sea salt

3 oz unsalted butter

2 small egg yolks

1–2 tablespoons cold water

2 lbs firm, ripe plums, pitted and quartered

Caster sugar to sprinkle

For the nut filling

2 oz toasted, coarsely ground hazelnuts

2 oz unsalted butter, softened

2 oz caster or granulated sugar

1 egg

*Serves 8–10 (In the photograph the tart shown was made
    using double quantities)*

Oven temperature: 450°F

To make the pastry, blend the dry ingredients and the butter to the texture of bread crumbs, either in a food processor or by hand. Add the egg yolks and just enough cold water to bind to a soft but not sticky dough. Wrap in plastic wrap and put it in the fridge to rest for 1 hour.

Roll out the pastry dough and line an 11 inch tart pan with it. Lightly prick over with a fork and chill.

Mix together the ingredients for the nut filling, and spread over the pastry. Cover the filling with plum quarters, butted against each other, and sprinkle with sugar. Bake in the preheated oven for 20–25 minutes until the skins of the plums are crisp at the edges and the plum juices are running.

PEARS POACHED IN MULLED WINE

This is a lovely recipe for when you have a glut of pears. Serve them with a dollop of crème fraîche or pouring custard.

6 firm, slightly ripe pears

1 lemon

1 bottle red wine

4 tablespoons clear honey

2 star anise

1 stick cinnamon

Serves 6

Peel the pears, keeping them whole and leaving the stalks intact. Using a potato peeler, peel the zest off the lemon in strips. Put the wine into a saucepan and stir in the honey, spices and lemon zest. Place the pears on their sides in the saucepan, making sure they are covered with the liquid. Bring to a boil, then simmer for about 20 minutes or until tender, turning them carefully so they color evenly. Lift the pears out and arrange on a dish. Bring the syrup back to a boil, and boil vigorously to reduce by half. Pour over the pears, complete with the lemon zest.

DAMSON SORBET

This is so simple, especially if made in an ice cream machine. It is an intensely flavored, wine-colored ice. Plums can be used instead of damsons, or almost any soft fruit you have such as blackcurrants or raspberries.

2 lbs damsons or plums

10 oz sugar

Juice of $\frac{1}{2}$ lemon if using plums

Serves 6

Stew the fruit whole with the sugar in a little water – up to $\frac{1}{2}$ cup – until soft. Sieve the pulp, then taste and add the lemon juice if needed. Following the instructions for your ice cream machine, if you are using one, pour the mixture into it slowly, while the paddle is moving so that it doesn't freeze up. Once it has finished churning, and if you are not eating at once, scoop out of the ice cream machine and freeze in another container.

If you have no ice cream machine, freeze in a tray and loosen up the mixture with a fork after 1 hour. Try to repeat this three times, continually refreezing the mixture.

61

OCTOBER

THE GARDEN AT THE BEGINNING of October flatters to deceive. The sun still has the heat to warm through your shirt, still carries the tang of summer during the middle of the day. But no one is fooled. This is not the real thing but borrowed from summer, little more than a good memory. Autumn has arrived. The leaves are changing color daily and the air has an almost tangible opacity you only find in autumn.

Because this is borrowed time, because the frosts will come any day, these days are as precious as jewels. It is too dark and cold to eat outdoors in the evening but there are still meals in the garden in the middle of the day. At its best, October sun and October light before the first frost are as beautiful as any other time in the garden. At the start of the month the flower borders still have their glowing richness that the frost will steal and are filled with russets and crimsons, purples and oranges, and the grass has an emerald intensity that is lost in the dry days of summer.

In the vegetable garden the last of the summer vegetables overlap winter ones like the leeks and cabbages that are now maturing fast. Tomatoes, sweet corn, Florence fennel, squashes and pumpkins ripen as a race against failing heat and light and, inevitably, all have to be collected in a spirit of compromise between saving what is good and accepting that some will not ripen at all.

But it is the fruit garden that really comes into its own. October in Herefordshire is dominated by apples. Even the main roads are reduced to a crawl by the stream of tractors pulling trailers filled with cider apples, collected by hand from trees 100 years old and more, being taken to the brewery in Hereford. Whole hillsides are busy as the commercial growers harvest their crop and our new orchard has its meager crop like oversized baubles on a Christmas tree. All our trees are standards and will grow to have stems a clear 6 feet tall before the first branch and, in the large trees like 'Bramley's', a canopy with a diameter of 20 feet or more when mature. But for now they are young and spindly and hardly more than a marker for the trees that they will become. Their fruit, however, grows as mature on these baby trees as on the most ancient one in the county. This is obvious but it took me rather by surprise the first year after I planted them with the flimsy branches bent double under the weight of the fruit – especially those with large cooking apples like 'Newton Wonder' and 'Bramley's'. Three trees had their leaders snapped in a high wind as a result, so in the second year I staked the leaders more securely and picked off all but a few fruits as they developed, leaving only those on strong lateral branches. This is one of the disadvantages of growing standard rather than bush trees, but one that is surely worth paying if you have the patience to wait a year or two.

We give the orchard its second cut of the year at the beginning of the month, raking up the long grass and then cutting it again with the collector. It is a big job, leaving two large blocks of composting grass and hay and one immaculate orchard with 55 young apple trees looking rather startled in their trim grass, shorn for the winter.

The 'Williams' pears growing as espaliers in the vegetable garden ripen at the beginning of the month and have to be checked daily to see that the wasps don't get to them first. Somewhere around the first week of the month they are all picked and put on the kitchen windowsill to ripen fully off the tree. Pears are precious in a way that is hard for an apple to be. This is because the perfect pear, eaten at the hour of ripeness with flesh that has a satin-smooth grain, bursting with juice and yet meltingly tender, is a rarity and so instantly recognizable as the definable thing that, once tasted, it becomes an obsession. Apples we take in all their variety, but all subsequent pears are judged by this absurdly high standard. I have to admit that none of my pears here at Ivington have come anywhere near perfection. But in our last garden we had an old 'Conference' pear that produced between 50 and 100 fruits each year, a quarter of which were very good indeed – even though 'Conference' is not reckoned to be among the finest of pears.

Autumn raspberries always seem much more of a treat than summer ones and are at their best in October, and the alpine strawberries go on producing their intense fruit up until the frosts. In our garden this is the month when we are most likely to get ripe figs – although much depends upon the weather throughout late summer.

October is never an easy ride. When the weather is good everything is fine but in the year of writing this book we had bad floods at the end of the month, reaching high into the garden, leaving cabbages bobbing about on the surface like buoys tethered by their stems and turning grass paths into hedge-lined canals. We love this. It is an annual treat that transforms our domain into a house at the edge of a great remote lake. Unfortunately, the water goes as fast as it arrives and leaves sludge and an astonishing amount of straw and dead vegetation behind, all of which has to be gathered up and put onto the compost heap. It also brings – as I have learned over the years – a new supply of nettle and dock seeds, which flourish in the sediment that millennia of this flooding have deposited.

The worst and most long-lasting effect of heavy winter rain is that it makes all our grass paths slimy on top and squishy beneath the surface. Walking on them makes it worse and wheeling a wheelbarrow reduces them to a quagmire. They stay this way except in hard frost until April and will not be reliably firm until the end of May. But when summer comes they look so good as freshly mown grass that we forget the inconvenience of them in winter till autumn comes around again.

Protection is the main concern at this time of year. The heated greenhouses are insulated with bubble wrap and the cold frames lined with 2-inch thick polystyrene sheeting (designed as underfloor insulation and very useful for all kinds of garden insulation). The cold greenhouse is cleared out completely and scrubbed down with disinfectant. It is then left with the doors and windows open so that it can disinfect and the chickens can get in to scratch around and eat as many slugs and bugs as possible. The tomatoes are all harvested first, with as many unripe green ones as red. There can be two or three wheelbarrows filled with tomatoes – as much as 155 lbs – to be processed at once. Most are frozen in the form of sauce, made with this year's onions, garlic and herbs. I don't mind the odd glut when you eat far more of one fruit or vegetable than normal for a month then do not taste it for a year, but there are very few things that cannot be stored or frozen to be eaten across the year.

The first of the 'Red Treviso' chicory is cut in mid-October. This has exquisite leaves looking exactly like a cockerel's tail feathers, green on the outside and deep bloodred within, the pattern repeating to the tiny heart leaves when split open. The radicchio is at its best, but with careful management it can be made to last through till spring. We cut it at the base and it regrows rapidly enough to ensure a second cut before Christmas. Cold rain rots the outer leaves, creating a moldy carapace, enveloping the inner ones which then start to rot as well, so we put cloches over them from October onward as a protection from the wet rather than the cold.

Just as most other summer-sown vegetables dissolve into soggy brownness, chicory starts to earn its keep. We grow 'Red Treviso', 'Grumulo Verde', 'Catalogna' chicory, variegated 'Castelfranco', 'Biondissima di Trieste', 'Selvatica di Campo' and the grasslike 'Minutina o Erba Stella'.

We do not blanch any chicory, but use the leaves specifically for their varying degrees of bitterness and allow for the fact that the outer leaves do blanch the inner ones very effectively. These outer leaves become weather worn by the end of autumn and have to be discarded, leaving perfectly protected hearts for cooking.

SUNDAY, OCTOBER 11:

Nice morning (but morning now is 8 AM).

Tied up cardoons with brown cardboard and weeded new vegetables.

Tidied and dug cardoons and artichokes.

CHARD

Chard comes into its own at the end of summer. We grow Swiss chard, with its green leaves and white stems; ruby chard, which has bright red stems and bronzed crimson leaves; and 'Jacob's Coat', which has stems ranging from white through yellow, pink and orange to magenta. Ruby chard is very good and the red very important to add winter color, but the standard Swiss chard is the best all-arounder if you have space for only one type.

Although it is sown in spring and germinates fast, chard is a slow, long-haul crop. There is always a point in each summer when I realize that we have not eaten any for weeks and I wonder why we are bothering to grow it. In September I know, because the white stalks are shining and clean and the leaves retain their freshness and billowing perkiness right into autumn. And it tastes very good.

The leaves cook and eat like a slightly coarse spinach and the stems like less stringy, less distinctively tasting celery. I am afraid that sells it short. As a rule, we eat our vegetables raw or cooked as unfussily as possible, putting all the emphasis into growing them well and eating them absolutely fresh. But chard's slight blandness means that both stalk and leaves will take a sauce very well.

Chard grows best on a rich soil, so add plenty of compost or manure, preferably in the autumn before sowing. The seed can be sown as early as March, but the soil must be sufficiently warm, so April is usually a better bet for us. The best plan is to sow two or three batches of seed in succession, each a month apart. You can sow it in plugs and then transplant the seedlings but I have found that there is little advantage in this: A row of seeds that were sown beside a row of young plants put out after being

grown under cover in plugs did just as well and matured just as fast – even though the seed was sown perhaps 40 days later. As soon as the seedlings are big enough to hold, thin them to 1 inch spacings and repeat the process a month later until there is at least 4 inches between each plant. This might seem generous but they will grow quite big.

Chard likes plenty of liquid, so never let it dry out. If you have plenty of organic matter in the soil, this should not be a problem except in an unduly dry season. If it does get too dry it will bolt and run to seed. Cut seeding stems right off as soon as you see them. In a very wet year the leaves may become brown and rotten; remove these, cutting the stem to the ground if need be. New leaves will grow back. Healthy plants should provide at least three fresh sets of leaves a year, from July through to the following May.

FRIDAY, OCTOBER 16:
Foul day – very wet, cold – horrible.
Cleared out top greenhouse, another wheelbarrow of
tomatoes – amazing indoor harvest.
Lots of peppers from two grow bags with 6 plants.

SQUASHES

There was a time when I thought that *squash* was a modern Americanization, connoting mushy fast food, and that in English squash could only be a game with a soft black ball, or too many people in an elevator. But this is ignorant, bigoted nonsense. A few years ago we started to grow squashes and pumpkins and were immediately entranced by them. As the Buddha nearly said – if you want to know it, grow it.

Marrows and zucchinis (or courgettes) are summer squashes by another name, and pumpkins, or squashes, are winter squashes. All are cucurbits, or gourds, as are melons. Squashes are among the oldest of fruits from the New World, every bit as venerable as potatoes, and their name, far from being the rather mushy invention I had ignorantly supposed, is derived from the Narraganset Indian word *askutasquash*, which means "a green thing eaten raw".

The first Puritan settlers, giving thanks for their first harvests, found that these fruits were at their best just at the beginning of autumn, and consequently squashes have become as much a part of Thanksgiving as turkey. It is a shame that we do not venerate them the same way here in the UK, because the fruits are incredibly beautiful with a wildly diverse range of sizes, shapes, colors and textures. And they taste fantastic as soup, chunks, mashed or in stews.

Squashes, however, are one of the few edible plants that are much easier to buy as seed and grow yourself than to buy from a store. They do take up room, but by the same token make superb short-term ground cover and will happily coexist with taller plants like sweet corn as long as they have rich, deeply dug soil for their roots to get into. We have grown yellow zucchini in among young artichokes and the two seemed to cohabit very well, the glaucal zigzagged leaves of the artichokes rising up from the dappled squash leaves and the brilliant chrome yellow sausages zinging up from the ground.

The ideal garden site for a squash plant is an old compost heap, which it will hide like a floral tea cozy while thriving in the rich, water-retentive growing medium. In open ground they need at least a square yard around them and, if you have the space, twice that amount, as their tentacle shoots will spread for yards if allowed. But their spreading season is short – between July and October – so can be fitted around other crops and flowering times. It is a good idea to dig a pit before planting, adding lots of manure and then refilling the topsoil and planting them in a slight crater so that water will funnel down to their roots.

One year we grew 'Turk's Turban', a white, beautifully fluted acorn variety whose name I forget but whose shape is identical to 'Ebony Acorn', 'Little Gem', whose skin is just like a summer squash's, and a round orange one called 'Baby Bear', all flanking the long, narrow artichoke walk. From the middle of August the path was completely lost in a sea of huge leaves and trailing stems of trifid vigor that manage to be brittle, succulent, bristly and hollow all at the same time. Frost hits these like a blowtorch, leaving the exposed fruit sitting on the ground like an abandoned clutch of monstrous eggs.

Acorn squashes are perhaps the best for most gardens, as they are not too huge, easy to grow and the orange ones are fantastic to eat. They have deeply fluted, smooth skin and vary from ivory to the richest orange, passing en route through green and an inky purple like fluted eggplants. There is something wonderful and rare about these solid, heavy objects in the hand, nourished primarily for the juicy flesh inside and yet feeling more like smooth stone than vegetable rind. Summer squashes are clumsy in comparison and, having eaten good winter squashes, it is hard to justify growing them. They are swollen symbols of the mushy, white-sauce-smothered culinary dessert of middle England. Hard-skinned squashes are meaty and rich in comparison. You can eat the growing tips, too.

However, a summer squash is merely a thin-skinned squash and the ones that ripen in late summer will keep – just like other squashes – for an astonishing length of time. Although a regular supply of water is essential, the main enemy of the maturing fruits is wet ground. This rots them and encourages slugs, which will eat into them before the rinds have a chance to thicken. Sunshine is needed for the skins to get thick and hard – the huge leaves shade the fruits, so it is important to let the squashes sit outside in the sun after the leaves die back to get as much sunlight as possible. This will improve their keeping qualities better than anything. Although they mature in autumn so that we associate the fruits with cool days and low light levels, squashes do not like cool conditions and absolutely hate cold soil.

Unless you have a heated propagator, the seeds will not germinate if it is cold, whatever the time of year. Therefore, May is early enough to sow them. They need heat of at least 60°F to germinate and must be kept dark. Make sure that the seed-starting medium is not cold and then sow them ½ inch deep on edge – the seeds are flat – two to a pot. Once both seeds have successfully germinated, remove the smaller of the two. They should be ready to plant out by midsummer. They then need about 100 days to flower, set fruit and ripen, which takes you through to the end of September. Forcing the pace is likely to prove fruitless.

SUNDAY, OCTOBER 18:

Frost overnight.

Killed back nasturtiums, squashes, artichokes, tomatoes, chicory, etc.

Lovely day – cold, bright.

SATURDAY, OCTOBER 24:

Rainy stormy day. Flooding very high.

Harvested sweet corn – very good. 36 cobs.

WEDNESDAY, OCTOBER 28:

Storm all night – 2in of rain.

Chickens out all night. One Plymouth hen missing.

Flood rose all day reaching new heights – (a) into yard, (b) reached hazel, (c) central path in kitchen garden under water, (d) bean bed under water, (e) all new vegetable garden, (f) main path at end of lime walk to chickens all under water.

Boiler, Aga, washing machines all down due to flood water on electrics, so:

No cooking

No heating

No hot water

No flushing toilet.

PUMPKIN SOUP

A thick creamy soup with the most amazing vivid orange color. If you are using a stock powder or bouillon cube, check before adding any extra salt.

1 small pumpkin (or part of a large one), about 1 lb 10 oz, skinned and cubed

2 medium-sized potatoes, peeled and cubed

1 tablespoon olive oil

2 cups stock

2 fresh tomatoes, chopped

4 fresh sage leaves

Sea salt and pepper

To garnish

18 large fresh sage leaves

Olive oil

Serves 6

Sweat the pumpkin and potato in the olive oil for 5 minutes in a saucepan. Add the stock, chopped tomatoes and sage leaves. Cover and simmer until the vegetables are soft (about 10 minutes). Purée until smooth, then gently reheat. Season to taste.

Add extra sage leaves, fried in olive oil until crisp, and serve immediately.

Making homemade pasta is undeniably more work than buying ready-made but very easy and much more fun. *Above left* The dough for ravioli is drawn through the pasta machine at decreasing thicknesses until it is in thin but malleable sheets. *Top right* It is then cut into squares. *Bottom right* The filling is spooned onto each square before another pasta square is placed over this to enclose it.

RAVIOLI FILLED WITH COTTAGE CHEESE AND CHARD

For the pasta dough

10 oz unbleached plain flour

Pinch of sea salt

2 eggs

3 egg yolks

Beaten egg to seal

For the filling

1 lb 5 oz chard

9 oz cottage cheese (or riccotta)

2 $\frac{1}{2}$ oz Parmesan cheese, freshly grated

$\frac{1}{4}$ nutmeg, freshly grated

Sea salt and pepper

To serve

Fresh Tomato Sauce (see page 56)

Freshly grated Parmesan cheese

Serves 6

To make the pasta, put the flour and salt in the food processor, and add the eggs and egg yolks, blending it all together until it starts to form a dough. If the mixture remains dry, add another egg yolk. Take the dough from the food processor and knead it on a floured surface for several minutes. Divide the dough into three or four separate balls, cover each in plastic wrap and let them rest in the fridge for an hour or two.

If you have a pasta machine, follow the manufacturer's instructions. If you don't, roll each piece out on a lightly floured surface, turning and folding it several times, until it becomes a smooth and malleable sheet. This is a bit of a performance, but it is very good fun. Do this in a cool place, and work as quickly as you can – you don't want the pasta to dry out. Finally, roll each sheet out as thinly and evenly as you can to make long strips about 7 inches wide. Trim the edges and cut into 6 inch squares. Keep the squares covered with plastic wrap.

To make the filling, strip the chard leaves and discard the stalks. Tear up the leaves and blanch for 3 minutes in boiling salted water. Drain well, squeezing out all excess water, then let it cool. Roughly chop the chard and mix with all the other filling ingredients.

Divide the filling into 24 equal balls and place one in the center of half of the pasta squares. Brush the edges with beaten egg and cover with another pasta square. Press firmly together around the edges to seal.

Place the ravioli in boiling salted water and simmer for 3–4 minutes. Serve three or four per person with Fresh Tomato Sauce and grated Parmesan.

STUFFED RAINBOW CHARD

These look more beautiful in the process than they do when they are cooked. The colors of the leaves and stalks are ravishing – vermilion, fuchsia, ocher, ruby red, brilliant green. Both the stalks and the leaves are edible, and can be cooked separately, but in this recipe they are both used.

6 large leaves of rainbow chard

Olive oil

For the stuffing

3 oz basmati rice

1 large onion, finely chopped

4 tablespoons olive oil

2 tablespoons pine nuts

2 tablespoons yellow raisins

Sea salt and pepper

Serves 6

Oven temperature: 375°F

Choose brightly colored stems of chard with similar-sized leaves. Wash the leaves thoroughly, and trim the stalk to about 2 inches. Keep and chop any leftover stalks.

Parboil the rice in salted water for about 5 minutes. Soften the onion in some of the olive oil. Add the chopped chard stalks and sweat for few more minutes. Mix all the stuffing ingredients together in a bowl.

Blanch the chard leaves for 1 minute in a large pan of boiling salted water. Drain and dry on kitchen paper. Lay a handful of stuffing mixture on the front of a leaf, then fold the edges over, and roll up into a parcel, ending with the stalk last. Secure with two wooden skewers that pass through the stalk.

Carefully pack the parcels into an oiled ovenproof dish. Pour in water to come about $1/2$ inch up the sides, and sprinkle olive oil over the parcels. Bake uncovered in the preheated oven for 25 minutes. Serve hot or warm.

CHARD WITH GARLIC IN OIL

Although this is so simple, it has a delicious silky texture, without the aftertaste of spinach, which I find too powerful.

2 heads chard or a small basketful from the garden
2 fat cloves garlic, roughly chopped
2 tablespoons olive oil
Large pinch of dried chili flakes
Lemon juice
Sea salt
Serves 6

Strip the chard leaves from the stems. Wash the leaves, leaving a little water clinging to them. Soften the garlic briefly in the olive oil, then stir in the chili flakes. Add the chard leaves and cook until they are soft but still bright green. Add lemon juice and salt to taste. Serve the chard on its own on toasted bread, or as part of a meal.

Variation Multicolored rainbow chard looks fantastic cooked like this – rich jewel-bright colors glistening with oil. Use small leaves whole, and blanch for a couple of minutes before tossing in the oil as above.

RUBY CHARD AND BEET RISOTTO

We eat variations on risotto several times a month. Our son Adam has cooked perfect plain risotto since he was eight; he is a patient cook and his method always works. This is the most fantastic color – deep purply red vegetables and bright orange rice.

2 medium beets, peeled and diced into $1/2$ in cubes
Olive oil
1 oz butter
1 red onion, chopped
2 cloves garlic, finely chopped
12 oz risotto rice
$1/2$ cup red wine
4 cups simmering vegetable or chicken stock
1 lb ruby chard, leaves and stems roughly chopped
Sea salt and pepper
Few sprigs of fresh thyme
Parmesan cheese
Serves 6

Gently sweat the beets in a small pan in a little olive oil for 5 minutes. Meanwhile, melt the butter in a deep straight-sided sauté pan and soften the onion, adding the garlic for the last minute or so. Add the rice and stir for a minute until glossy. Add the beets and the red wine, and simmer. When the rice has absorbed the wine, start to add the stock, one ladleful at a time. Each time, let the stock be absorbed before adding more. Stir continuously but very gently – do not break up the rice grains. About 5 minutes before the end of cooking, remove the pan from the heat and add the ruby chard. Stir it into the risotto, then return to the heat and finish cooking for 5 minutes, stirring gently. Season with salt, pepper and thyme just before serving with freshly grated Parmesan cheese.

Variation If the beets have nice healthy leafy tops, you can shred these and stir them in at the last minute.

PIGEON STUFFED WITH CHARD

Pigeons are at their very best in autumn, fattened from gleaning corn, and are a bargain in the market, dressed and trussed. Chard is a very useful vegetable, and is here used to give a slightly sharp, bitter flavor to the stuffing for the birds.

6 plump pigeons (1 per person)

Sea salt and pepper

Butter

2 tablespoons olive oil

Red wine (approximately $\frac{1}{3}$ bottle)

2 teaspoons redcurrant jelly or Damson Cheese
   (see page 57)

For the stuffing

6 chard leaves

Grated zest of 1 lemon

Bread crumbs from $\frac{1}{2}$ loaf white bread, (about 5 oz)

4 oz butter

2 oz pine nuts

2 oz yellow raisins

Serves 6

Oven temperature: 375°F

Clean and dry the pigeons, and salt and pepper the cavities. Make the stuffing by finely shredding the chard, having taken out the midribs. Chop the midribs separately. Mix together all the stuffing ingredients. Loosely stuff the cavities of the birds, dot them with butter and wrap in waxed paper. Put in a roasting pan and bake in the preheated oven for 35 minutes. They can then be roasted uncovered, in which case keep them basted with the olive oil and red wine.

Use the juices in the roasting pan to make a rich sauce, with the redcurrant jelly or Damson Cheese and a little more wine, stirring over a moderate heat on top of the cooker to reduce a little and scraping up any cooking juices on the bottom of the roasting pan.

APPLE AND QUINCE JELLY

$2\frac{1}{4}$ lbs cooking apples or crab apples

$2\frac{1}{4}$ lbs quinces

$6\frac{1}{2}$ cups water

$4\frac{1}{2}$ lbs sugar (approximately)

Makes about ten 1 lb jars

Wash the fruit and cut up into quarters. Put into a large preserving pan and cover with the water. Bring to a boil, then simmer until the fruit is soft.

Strain the liquid from the fruit through a jelly bag. Allow it to drip through; be patient. Don't squeeze the bag or the jelly will be cloudy.

Warm the sugar in a low oven to help it dissolve quickly. Put your sterilized jam jars into the oven to warm through.

Measure the quantity of liquid into the clean preserving pan and add $2\frac{1}{4}$ lbs of warm sugar to each $5\frac{1}{2}$ cups of juice. Reheat slowly, stirring to make sure the sugar has dissolved before the liquid begins to boil. Let it boil vigorously for a few minutes. Test to see if it has set by putting a drop onto a cold saucer; leave to cool, then push the side of the drop with your finger to see if it wrinkles. If it is still runny it needs to boil longer. When the jelly has reached setting point, allow it to cool a little before pouring into the warm jam jars and sealing them with waxed circles and cellophane.

APPLE CHARLOTTE

This should be made in a metal charlotte mold that has sloping sides and two little handles. The buttered bread crisps up on the outside, contrasting with the sweet pulpy inside.

3 lbs 3oz cooking apples or mixed cooking and
    eating apples
5 oz butter
5 oz sugar
Juice of 1 lemon
Pinch of cinnamon
12 thin slices dry white bread
Serves 6
Oven temperature: 375°F

Peel, core and slice the apples. Melt 2 oz of the butter in a pan over a gentle heat, and add the apples. Add a little water to stop the apples from sticking, and cook gently until the apples have softened. Stir in the sugar, lemon juice and cinnamon, then take off the heat.

Melt the remaining butter. Dip each slice of bread in the butter on both sides, then use most of the slices to line a 4½-cup charlotte mold. Fill the mold with the apple pulp and use the rest of the buttered bread slices to make a lid.

Bake in the preheated oven for about 45 minutes, when the surface will be golden brown. Serve with Pouring Custard (see page 173).

Variation This can be made in individual metal molds rather than one large one, in which case the baking time will be reduced to about 25 minutes.

TARTE TATIN

The French serve this with a very bitter top and very sweet pastry. Early in the season we use dessert apples for apple pies and cooking apples later in the year when they in turn are sweeter. This means we can keep the pastry less sweet to avoid masking the fruitiness of the apple. But *chacun à son gout*. You can substitute pears for the apples.

For the pastry
6 oz unbleached plain flour
3 oz unsalted butter
1 egg yolk
1 teaspoon caster or granulated sugar
1–2 tablespoons cold water
For the filling
10 medium-sized apples
For caramelizing the apples
4 oz unsalted butter
3 oz granulated sugar
Serves 6
Oven temperature: 375°F

Make a pastry dough in a food processor from the flour, butter, egg yolk, sugar and water. Allow it to rest in the refrigerator for 30 minutes before rolling out.

Peel, quarter and core the apples. Melt the unsalted butter and granulated sugar in a pan that can also be used in the oven. Add the apples and toss to coat with the butter and sugar mixture, then cook on a moderate heat until they are soft – about 10 minutes. Increase the heat to high to caramelize the apples.

Roll out the pastry to the same size as the pan and cover the apples, carefully pressing it down around the sides of the fruit. Bake in the preheated oven for 35 minutes. Cool for 5 minutes, then turn out upside down on a serving plate.

TARTE TATIN

NOVEMBER

NOVEMBER IS THE MONTH when the garden closes in on itself, becoming introverted and almost truculent in its inaccessibility. The clocks have gone back and the garden closes down. It never fails to astonish me how fast the light fades away at this end of the year. Much of this is due to the unfamiliarity of winter – we have gotten used to summer and have been seduced into a gentle dying away by autumn, so the stark realization that we are in winter is always a shock.

The garden shrivels. Flower borders reduce down to a fraction of their summer selves, hedges are stripped bare or, like our hornbeams, hang on to tatters and shreds of their leaves, rustling in the wind with a sound that is exactly like the first drops of rain.

The vegetable garden loses much – the rhubarb leaves fall away to nothing, all beans have to be removed, leaves of roots such as parsnips and carrots reduce dramatically – but it can be the strongest and most vital part of the garden at this time of year. The brassicas, which for us mean savoys, cavolo nero, red cabbage, purple sprouting broccoli and an early Dutch cabbage, take over a central decorative role. Anyone who thinks of cabbages as boring has never seen them grow in early winter. We plant them out in blocks and it is as much the repetition of shape and color as the individual qualities of any one plant that achieves the satisfyingly decorative effect.

The savoys are as intense a green as euphorbia in spring, ranging from a yellow glow to the powdery blue that is characteristic of the whole brassica family at this time of year. Cavolo nero tastes much better after a frost (as do parsnips) and the depth of their green makes the title of

POTATO CAKES

The second of these two recipes for potato cakes I like to serve with pigeon.

1 lb floury potatoes, cooked and cooled
1 tablespoon finely chopped fresh chives
Sea salt and pepper
Unbleached plain flour for shaping
Butter for cooking
Serves 6

Mash the potatoes with the chives and salt and pepper to taste. With lightly floured hands, take small balls of mashed potato and pat into flat cakes. This quantity should make approximately 12 cakes.

The cakes are meant to be cooked on a preheated cast-iron griddle, but a heavy frying pan greased with a little butter will do. Cook the cakes for 2 minutes on each side until browned.

Lift them very carefully – because there is no binding agent, they are quite fragile.

DICED ROAST POTATOES IN OLIVE OIL

This is one that the children love. I don't cook french fries, so to me this is the nearest thing to them. Either 'Belle de Fontenay' or 'Ratte' potatoes are good for this because their waxy texture holds the shape.

We had to dig up the entire potato crop early one year because of blight. We were left with lots of tiny potatoes, particularly 'Ratte' and 'Pink Fir Apple', about 2–3 inches long. They are narrow little sausage-shaped potatoes, so to use them up they were sliced in half and cooked this way – even more like french fries.

1 ½ lbs waxy potatoes

2–3 tablespoons olive oil

Sea salt

Fresh rosemary, finely chopped

Serves 6

Oven temperature: 450°F

Wash the potatoes, leaving the skins on as these varieties are often small. Dice into ½ inch cubes. Spread the potatoes out in a single layer in a large, flat metal baking pan – you may need two – and toss with the olive oil to coat. Roast for about 15 minutes; they are ready when soft inside and slightly crisp and golden brown outside. Sprinkle with sea salt and rosemary just before serving.

BAKED SAUSAGES

It is so important to know where your meat comes from. A Ludlow butcher I like names the farm that his meat comes from, and I have faith in his integrity. Pork butchers locally take pride in their secret recipes for handmade sausages. Little chipolatas are a perfect size for children who refuse to eat big fat sausages. Sausages have to be meaty, and without gristly bits and bone, otherwise I am completely put off – I would never touch the pink industrial numbers. Cooked slowly in the oven rather than fried, the texture of

the sausage improves and is somehow tastier, but take care not to let them dry out.

1 ½ lbs chipolatas

Serves 6

Oven temperature: 375°F

Cut the sausages apart and arrange on a lightly oiled baking tray. Bake in the preheated oven for 20–30 minutes. Serve with good Dijon mustard and Bread Sauce (see page 88).

868 6

ROAST PHEASANT

Pheasants are plentiful in the autumn. The pheasant season is October to February, and the birds are at their best from November to January. A brace of pheasants (a male and a female) costs us about eight dollars, all beautifully dressed, lying side by side, waiting to be cooked.

There are two ways I cook pheasant, either in the traditional manner with fried bread crumbs or with slices of apple softened in butter. They can be dry as they have little fat of their own, so they need a bit of help.

Brace of dressed pheasants
Fresh thyme
Sea salt and pepper
2 oz butter
6 strips streaky bacon
2 apples, such as 'Russets', 'Cox's' or 'Newton Wonder'
Serves 4–6
Oven temperature: 375°F

Stuff the cavity of each bird with a generous bunch of thyme, a little salt and pepper, and a pat of butter. Rub butter over the breast, and wrap with the streaky bacon. Roast in the preheated oven, basting from time to time. After 40–45 minutes, lift the birds on to a hot plate and keep warm.

Peel and core the apples and cut into thick slices. Cook gently in the roasting juices on top of the stove until caramelized – 5–10 minutes.

Variation For fried crumbs and gravy instead of apple, use an equal weight of butter to dried bread crumbs – approximately 4–6 oz. Although this sounds very rich, the result is light and crunchy, and the crumbs absorb the gravy. Fry the bread crumbs in the butter until light brown and crisp. Serve with gravy made from the roasting juices, a splash of wine or cider, a little apple or redcurrant jelly and a little water if it needs thinning. Strain and serve.

RABBIT WITH MUSTARD

Wild rabbits are inexpensive in local markets. Only buy them when there is an *r* in the month. These animals have no spare fat and are muscly, but if they are cooked slowly the meat becomes tender. The meat is like a cross between chicken and game – pale in color but with a gamey texture.

2 rabbits, jointed
Seasoned unbleached plain flour
$\frac{1}{2}$ oz butter
1 tablespoon oil
3 red onions, quartered
1 cup cider
Handful of fresh thyme
Handful of fresh oregano
1 cup vegetable stock
2 tablespoons Dijon mustard
Sea salt
Handful of fresh parsley, finely chopped
Serves 6
Oven temperature: 375°F

Either buy the rabbits whole and joint them, or if you find their appearance alarming, ask your butcher to do this for you. Coat the rabbit pieces in seasoned flour. Heat the butter and oil in a flameproof casserole and fry the rabbit pieces for 10 minutes until browned on all sides. Remove to a warm plate. Cook the onions in the same fat until slightly caramelized. Return the rabbit to the casserole, pour in the cider and boil rapidly until the liquid is reduced by half. Scatter over the thyme and oregano and add the vegetable stock. Cover and bake in the preheated oven for 1 hour or more until tender. Strain off the sauce, stir in the mustard and taste for seasoning. Pour over the rabbit and serve, sprinkled with parsley.

Variation For a richer sauce a cupful of heavy cream can be stirred into the sauce after the mustard and brought to a boil just before serving.

FREYA'S BREAD SAUCE

I like to think of bread as a medieval thickening agent in the kitchen. Our daughter loves sloppy food and insists on bread sauce with sausages. This is her recipe (but as a treat she prefers to have sauce made from a package).

1 medium-sized onion

6 cloves

1 1/2 cups whole milk

Bread crumbs from 1/2 loaf of day-old white bread, about 5 oz

Sea salt and pepper

Freshly grated nutmeg

Pat butter

Serves 6

Peel the onion, but leave it whole, and stud with the cloves. Steep the onion in the milk, gently warming it for 30 minutes. Add the bread crumbs and heat together, stirring everything so it doesn't come to a boil and burn. Take off the heat and leave in a warm place for 30 minutes for the sauce to thicken. Season with salt, pepper and nutmeg, and stir in a knob of butter for extra richness. Freya leaves in the onion for the flavor to develop, but most experts say you should remove it. It is up to you.

STEAMED APPLE PUDDING

This is basic stick-to-your-ribs English cooking, but when you break open the pudding the spicy perfume of the quince raises it to another level.

For the pastry

5 oz fresh unsalted butter or vegetable shortening

10 oz unbleached plain flour

Cold water to bind

For the filling

1 lb apples, such as 'Newton Wonder' or 'Bramley's'

1 quince (or pinch of ground cinnamon and 2 cloves)

3 oz sugar

4 tablespoons water

Serves 6

Make the pastry by rubbing the butter or shortening with the flour or mixing the ingredients in a food processor. Use enough water to give a soft, elastic dough.

Grease the inside of a 4-cup pudding dish. Reserve enough pastry to make the lid. Roll out the remainder to about 5/8 inch thick in a circle to go up the sides of the dish, gathering it to make it fit.

Peel, core and finely slice the apples and the quince. Layer the fruit in the dish, sprinkling each layer with sugar (and cinnamon, if used). Pack the fruit in, to the top of the basin (add the cloves, if using). Add the water. Roll out the remaining dough to make a lid. Seal the lid, trim the edges and cover with two layers of greased waxed paper, folded in a pleat to allow for expansion. Stand the basin on a clean white muslin cloth, and tie alternate corners together tightly over the waxed paper to hold it firmly in place.

Lower the pudding into a saucepan of boiling water. The water should come about halfway up the side of the dish. Reduce the heat so the water is simmering and cover the pan. Keep checking the water level and top it off from a boiling kettle as necessary throughout the cooking period. The pudding will be cooked in 3 hours.

DECEMBER

TWO OF OUR CHILDREN have their birthdays in December, and there is Christmas and New Year's Eve – and other than these entirely nonhorticultural events, December has little to recommend it. By the shortest day, December 21, it is not light enough to begin work outside until 8:30 AM and too dark to go on past 4:30 PM. Consequently, it is the month when we do the least gardening of all. Days go by with no outdoor activity. Just walking to feed the chickens can create soggy foot holes in the grass, and the cultivated ground is usually far too wet to tread on.

But December always has a very mild spell, often around Christmas, which is less welcome than snow or ice. Mild weather with no light means a gray dampness in this part of the world. Global warming here in England is turning out to mean warm, wet winters and cool, wet summers. Winter

warmth does no good at all to the garden or to most humans with the means to keep themselves warm. Harmful insects, fungi and vermin increase without check and the plant growth that occurs in this warmth is sappy and tender – and hit by the first cold spell when it does happen.

One way to cheer yourself up when surrounded by midwinter gloom is to read nursery catalogs and plant lists and plan for a sunlit spring and summer. The other is to have made sure that there is plenty still in the garden to bring to the table. In summer this is easy. But in winter it takes some planning.

At the beginning of the month the last of the apples can be picked from the trees. 'Newton Wonder', 'Bramley's Seedling', 'King of the Pippins' and 'William Crump' will still be on the tree in our orchard. These apples store well and are cookers that can be used for solidly comforting winter puddings like apple pie, steamed apple pudding, apple charlotte and baked apple. There is something trusty and potatolike about a large cooking apple: It is almost something for the pantry rather than a fruit. It is a means to an end that is as appley as the freshest eater off the tree, but only cooking releases this. This kitchen will have been filled with the smell of cooked apples in the dead of winter ever since it was built, 500 years ago. The 'Herefordshire Pearmain' (which is a dessert apple) was grown then, and grows now in our orchard, as was the 'Costard', which is now extinct, but would have cooked here on this fire.

They would have added quince to their pies then, just as we do now. Quinces are picked in autumn but can sit as a pomander in a bowl, scenting the room sweetly as any flower, their woolly, waxy skins preventing the fruit from withering for months.

Quinces are a lovely fruit, of a beautifully warm yellow and a wonderful fragrance. Quince immeasurably improves apple in any form, makes wonderful jelly and custard and was the original marmalade, the Portuguese preserve made from quinces being called *marmelo*. Edible quinces will grow from a decorative *Chaenomeles*, but much better are the quinces from the rarer quince tree, *Cydonia oblonga*, grown purely for the fruit. Quinces grow slowly into a compact but proper tree and like wet ground, so are ideal for the banks of a pond or stream. I have planted four here, 'Champion', 'Lescoviz', 'Vranja' and 'Portugal', in a place near the margins of the garden that regularly floods so they can get the dampness they like. They grow as scruffy, unruly trees, resisting pruning and organization, and are all the more lovable for that.

Jewish mythology has it that the forbidden fruit in the garden of Eden was not an apple, but quince, the quintessential fruit of good and evil. With their broad-hipped shape they are a sexy fruit and were considered an emblem of love. In Mediterranean countries brides would eat one before retiring to the bridal bed, properly fortified for the nuptial rites.

From the vegetable garden red cabbage and savoy cabbages are ready for cutting, and cavolo nero for picking. Chicory of all kinds is at its best. Rocket, mizuna, corn salad and radicchio should provide leaves enough for a daily salad. Stored pumpkins and squashes should retain their viability if they have been exposed to sunshine for a few weeks after harvest and kept cool and dry, and celeriac, celery, parsnips, carrots, turnips and beets can remain in the ground to be dug as necessary. The leeks that were planted in July are large enough for using, although the later ones will not fill out until into the New Year. Garlic should be planted either as the main crop or as a second or third sowing to get a succession.

CHICORY

The most exciting crop that we draw upon in December is chicory. This is a fairly recent departure for us, not least because chicory seed has been difficult to find until the past few years. However, it is now widely available and no more difficult to grow than lettuce – but without the threat of it running to seed. It is worth any amount of trouble to get the seed because it is ideally suited to a northern climate, grows easily and has an addictive, bitter piquancy that is particularly good when cooked and eaten with meat or fish.

All chicories are simplicity itself to grow. They need a long growing season but do not germinate well in cold soil, so either cover the soil to warm it up or wait until it is not cold to touch – which for us is not before May. Seed varies enormously from variety to variety with some having a corky character and others being very fine indeed, but sow all types thinly in rows. I have tried sowing 'Grumulo' chicory broadcast but this only works in ground that is absolutely free of weeds and I see little advantage in it. Thin the plants as they grow, otherwise they will not develop good hearts – which is the primary reason for growing them. The thinnings are very good in salads. Chicory needs plenty of water, so do not let it dry out, although all types have a tendency to get slimy if standing in the wet; you may need to protect it from the rain with row covers in very wet weather.

Chicory grows in two stages, developing a strong root and producing green leaves, which are very good in salads, especially when they are young. In late summer these leaves change form; some varieties die right back and then regrow and some varieties change color, turning bright red in response to cold and lower light levels. Some varieties have a kind of self-blanching mechanism where the outer leaves protect the inner ones from light, which results in these being paler and less bitter.

This bitterness is a defining feature of chicory. It adds depth to the otherwise almost ubiquitous sweetness of leaf vegetables. Also, many chicories develop strong leaf stems that are too tough to be eaten raw but cook very well. All in all, they are an important element in the vegetable garden, particularly in winter.

Traditionally, the English vegetable gardener has grown witloof chicory for its blanched chicons. These can be delicious but are a performance to produce and by no means the best chicory that you can eat. To get the white chicons you must grow the chicory all summer so that it establishes a strong root system, then in autumn cut off the head – which looks like a shaggy lettuce – flush with the soil. If the weather is mild, it can be blanched by placing a flower pot over it and putting straw down that to keep it from freezing. Traditionally, it is dug up a few roots at a time, trimmed and then potted up in peat or sand, a pot inverted over it and put in a warm, dark place so that the new leaves grow back white. When these are of sufficient size to cut, the root is discarded.

However, we now grow a number of chicories to be eaten both in salads in the summer and for cooking in winter. These include 'Variegata di Chioggia', which has green leaves speckled with red, and 'Red Treviso', which, if

I had to choose only one chicory to grow, is the best because it has the most beautiful red leaves growing from the ground that look exactly like cockerel feathers. These develop only after the first flush of leaves, which are looser and green, has died back in autumn and then the interior turns deep burgundy, while the outside leaves remain green – as striking and rich as any fine garment. After this the new leaves all emerge red.

'Red Treviso' has an extraordinarily deep taproot, so can either be cut at ground level – in which case, new leaves will grow – or must be dug deeply. 'Red Verona' has lovely red leaves looser than radicchio and less upright than 'Red Treviso'. 'Grumulo Verde' is the toughest of all chicories, surviving any weather and growing almost perennially. It also has two leaf forms, starting out loose leaved and then developing round, almost spiraled heads. 'Catalogna' chicory can be grown as 'Catalogna Brindisina' primarily for the stalks or puntarelles (flowering stems) that it grows the spring following planting, or for its stems and leaves, as with 'Catalogna a Foglia Fastagliata'. Both of these look quite like a dandelion when growing, with large, deeply serrated leaves. We also grow a diminutive chicory called 'Minutina o Erba Stella', which at first looks like grass or flat chives as it grows throughout the summer, but in autumn and over winter it develops the typical chicory heart and leaf stems so that you can cut or dig up the entire plant and cook it whole. It is very good. The most familiar chicory to most people is radicchio, mainly because it can be eaten raw without too much bitterness. However, it is also exceptionally good cooked.

Other than the puntarelle, or flowering stem, all these chicories are best eaten by digging them up whole, trimming the roots off, leaving a collar at the base of the leaves so that they all stay attached.

I sow all the chicories from late spring to midsummer in a rich, well-prepared site. They prefer light soil and good drainage but are tough and adaptable. Sow them in rows and keep them well weeded and watered. Thin them as they grow, using the thinnings in salads. There is something to be said for growing them in plugs or seed trays and then transplanting them, which makes for better germination and final spacing. The idea is to have them all at least 6 inches apart by the time you go into autumn.

Chicories are largely untroubled by cold, but will rot in wet weather, developing a carapace of soggy, rotting leaves that have to be removed to reveal a perfectly healthy interior. I find that row covers, left open at the ends, are ideal if the weather is very wet.

ENDIVE

Endive is a member of the chicory family, although it is less bitter, and the most commonly grown is the curly- or frizzle-leaved kind, grown in conjunction with lettuce and used as part of summer salads. However, endive is much tougher than lettuce and, if protected by straw, a row cover or mulch, can easily last into December. The broad-leaved varieties such as 'Cornet de Bordeaux' or a hardier, curly-leaved one like 'Coquette' or 'Frisée de Ruffec' are tougher and better for winter standing.

I sow them in early August, along with rocket, mizuna, 'Winter Density' lettuce and 'All the Year Round' lettuce, and corn salad, to provide the leaves for winter salads. For this kind of sowing that is time-critical I have gotten into the habit of sowing half of the seed packet outside where they are to grow, and the other half in seed trays in the greenhouse. These latter are a safety net in case of poor germination or attack from slugs, ensuring the right spacing of 6 inches when transplanted a month or so later.

The young seedlings at this late-summer/early-autumn period are much less vigorous than their spring counterparts and therefore less easy to sacrifice. By sowing or planting at a wide spacing, very little thinning is required so more of the precious winter harvest survives. Endives are prone to rot like other chicories, so will need protection in very damp weather.

RED CABBAGE

You cannot have too much red in a vegetable garden. I have extolled the obvious virtues of red chicories, and now it is the turn of red cabbage. Actually, red cabbage is as blue as it is red, the outer leaves developing a blue bloom as the rain and cold works on them, diluting the anthocyanin pigments and washing out the red. As hardy as anything, its purple-gray globes will sit ready for eating all winter, whatever the vagaries of the weather.

Red cabbage is very good slowly stewed with juniper, brown sugar and vinegar, making a good accompaniment to game, particularly venison. Now, however delicious, there is not a huge calling for red cabbage in the Don household, with the children looking at it with only slightly less hostility than boiled rat, so I only grow one packet of seeds of one variety, 'Red Dutch'. Nevertheless, this will provide a couple of dozen big cabbages for Sarah and myself and anyone else who wants to join in.

They are sown in the outdoor seedbed in May at the same time as the savoy cabbages and planted in late July or early August at about 12 inch spacings. They will last until the ground is needed in March or April, when they are best followed by a root crop such as parsnips, carrots or beets (but not turnips, rutabagas or radishes, which are all of the same brassica group as the red cabbage and therefore liable to any disease that it may have been harboring).

PARSNIPS

Parsnips have a long gestation, belonging exclusively to winter. They need a frost to intensify the sugars in them. But they grow slowly, underground and out of sight, for six months before harvesting.

They have been grown in the UK since the Romans introduced them and were very widely eaten before the potato became the staple starchy vegetable. They are currently undervalued, perhaps because they are not quick and instant. I can't see McDonald's doing a line in parsnip fries – although there is no reason why not. They will

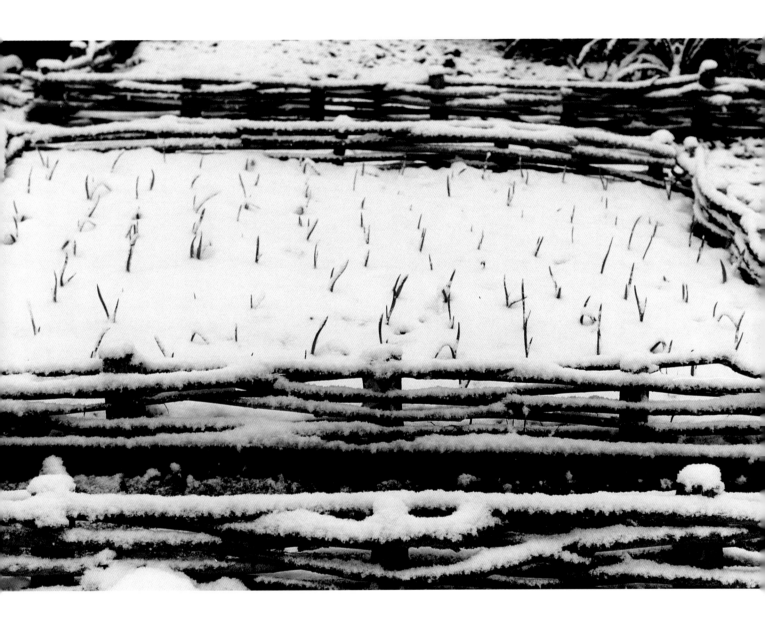

Garlic leaves peeking through the snow. Although an archetypal Mediterranean plant, garlic is very tough and needs a certain amount of cold weather to develop a good head of cloves, which is why it is planted in midwinter.

withstand any amount of foul weather and will stay unharmed in the ground until you want to eat them, unlike carrots, which need to be lifted soon after the first frosts. There is something reliable and immensely satisfying about digging along a row, perhaps marked only by a few wisps of leaves after a winter of rain and frost, and extracting half a dozen muddy white cones tapering to a tail.

They are not at all difficult to grow but the large, flat seeds are slow to germinate and are best sown in April on a piece of ground that will not be needed for a year. The soil must be dug to a good depth if the roots are to develop to any size, although varieties such as 'White Gem' and 'Gladiator' have shorter, broader roots and so are better suited to heavy ground. But all parsnips like a light, well-drained soil best. For the roots to swell they must be able to push aside the soil around them, and compacted, heavy soil makes this difficult.

They are very good roasted, especially alongside a roast beef, so that the outside is crisp and the inside a lovely sweet goo. But the most popular way of eating them in our family is as a purée.

CELERY

When I was a child celery seemed to be a regular feature of every vegetable garden in the village (the extent of my world), and certainly our household ate it often raw, always served with the stalks in a jar filled with water. We ate it with cold meat, mashed potato and chutney on Mondays and with Stilton at Christmas. We also had it hot as part of the stews and casseroles that featured very heavily in my mother's cuisine, as well as poached or braised, and the leaves were chopped and added as flavoring to soups. I liked it then and I like it now, but my impression is that it is not so commonly grown or used today as it was over a quarter of a century ago.

Perhaps it is because it is perceived to be difficult to grow or prepare in the kitchen – neither of which is justified. Celery stalks that are not blanched are much

tougher and less tasty. We grow both self-blanching and trench celery. Self-blanching celery is grown in blocks so that the plants shield one another from light. Trench celery is planted in a trench that is then backfilled to stop the light reaching them, thereby blanching them.

Trench celery can also be grown on the surface and each plant individually blanched with brown paper, newspaper or black polythene tied around it with string. I have tried this but it is a terrible challenge, as well as providing the perfect haven for slugs. Better to stick to a trench. The great advantage of trenched celery is that it tastes better and has a longer season, whereas self-blanching celery does not like hard frosts.

The seed is sown in seed trays in March or April in the greenhouse. Separate the seedlings out after about three weeks into another seed tray or large plugs. Keep the seedlings well watered and do not expose to a temperature of less than 50°F for more than 12 hours, otherwise they are liable to bolt before they mature. In practice, this means not being in a hurry to plant the seedlings out and keeping them in a cold frame or greenhouse until mid-May, or covering the seedlings if there is a cold spell.

At the time of sowing, dig over the ground that will be used for self-blanching celery, adding in extra organic material such as mushroom compost. For trench celery, dig a trench about 18 inches wide and 12 inches deep. Loosen the bottom thoroughly with a fork and mix in plenty of well-rotted organic material, filling back with the topsoil to within 6 inches of the top. Leave the residue banked up on either side of the trench; you will use it later in the season to draw around the growing stalks.

Plant out the young celery in mid-May, in a single row in the trench or in blocks for self-blanching, each plant about 12 inches apart in both instances. It is a good idea to grow them near celeriac and to water all very thoroughly, at least once a week. Not only will water improve the growth but also the more succulent celery is, the better it tastes. When I was a child we always used to sprinkle the trench with soot, as an anti-slug device, I think. Soot is in short supply nowadays. Keep well weeded and earth up the trenched celery every month or so, drawing the soil with a hoe or spade so that only the top leaves stick out. Before you earth up, take the side shoots off – you can tie the stalks of each plant up first but I don't bother. It is a good idea to remove the side shoots of self-blanching celery, too, although the inner plants in the block are harder to get at and will usually be okay if left alone.

Start using self-blanching celery from September, primarily to eat cooked. Trench celery is ready from October and should last well into the New Year, although very hardy varieties like the pink-stemmed 'Giant Red' will last the longest.

THURSDAY, DECEMBER 10:
Fox took four hens overnight. Searched common but found no bodies.

On Christmas Day we traditionally eat a goose, bought from the farm across the fields on the side of the hill. It is run by a family that has grazed geese there for Christmas for 50 years. Until recently, they also prepared geese for Michaelmas (September 29) but there is no longer any call for them. It used to be normal that the farmer's wife tended chickens and geese to sell eggs and the birds as an important part of her household income. When Sarah and I lived for a year on the North York moors, our neighboring farm had a flock of geese that terrorized any passerby, racing at them with craning necks, cackling. Geese have a sharp peck and are aggressive. But they are part of the rhythm of the landscape, lined across the fields beneath a white winter sky, and wonderful to eat as a seasonal treat. But it is certain that gradually the flocks will disappear, as farmers and their wives retire and a gaggle of geese will not fit into the management scheme of a young farming couple.

We try to eat simply at Christmas and not get sucked into the surfeit of overrich food, but nevertheless make a genuine feast of it. In the week before Christmas we make raised pies and mince pies. Christmas pudding has been made months, if not years, earlier.

On Christmas morning we drink champagne for breakfast. That is the culinary bit the children like best. The goose is stuffed with local apples (in a year or two they will come from our orchard) and roasted. It is such a rich bird and the taste so strong that it does not need a mass of accompaniments, side dishes or sauces. Just lightly cooked cabbage and simple roast potatoes (tricky when the main-crop potatoes are ravaged by blight, but we had a good crop of red 'Duke of York's' that did well) and, of course, the apples that it was stuffed with. A dry local organic cider is the best drink to go with it.

The week after Christmas is always a good time in the garden – a time to take stock, do much walking around, thinking and planning, as well as digging and planting trees and hedges provided the weather allows. If the first three weeks of December are the absolute nadir of the year, by the end of the month there is a strong sense of survival. We have come through.

THURSDAY, DECEMBER 31:
Damp, gray, mild day.
This has been officially the warmest year ever recorded, and the wettest, coldest and most miserable for a very long time in my own subjective experience. It has been a hard year to garden in, the ground sodden, spring very cold, snails and slugs in plaguelike proportions.
Never had enough time to do what I had to – let alone what I wanted – yet, on balance, the garden was better than ever – better tended, better flowered, better structured (huge improvement here, hedges really maturing) and better for food.
New greenhouses and cold frames a vast improvement.
I planted garlic and pruned the trees in the orchard.
And so our garden year ended.

ROAST GOOSE STUFFED WITH APPLES

This is our Christmas feast. I order the goose from a local farm. It is traditional for farmers' wives locally to fatten geese for Michaelmas and the Christmas market. It is lovely to see the beautiful white birds in the fields and orchards as you drive past, and know that one of them will be your Christmas meal. I collect it, plucked, trussed and prepared, on the day before Christmas Eve, with its fresh gleaming liver tucked under its wing. We keep the snowy white goose fat to use in cooking for the rest of the year. The best roast potatoes are cooked in goose fat. It is best to drink a dry local cider with this.

10–12 lb goose

2 lbs medium-sized cooking apples, peeled, halved and
    cored

Sea salt and pepper

1 tablespoon apple jelly

Serves 6–8 (with leftovers)

Oven temperature: (to start) 450°F

(then) Medium, 375°F

First prepare your goose by pouring a large kettle of boiling water over it as it sits in the sink. This is supposed to loosen the skin and make it crispier.

Season the cavernous cavity of the goose, then very simply stuff the cavity with the apples, salted and peppered. Or use the stuffing recipe that follows. Put the goose on a rack above a deep roasting pan and roast in the preheated hot oven for 30 minutes. Check and baste regularly, every 10 minutes or so. Reduce the oven temperature to medium and continue to roast for 2 1/2–3 hours. Continue the basting, and now and then gently prod the skin all over with a fork to allow the fat to run, being careful not to stick the fork into the meat or the juices will run out. Check to see that the meat is cooked by putting a skewer or a sharp knife between the leg and the breast – if the juice runs clear, it is ready. If it is still pink, cook the goose for a little longer.

After 2 hours of cooking, take some of the goose fat to roast potatoes to accompany the meal.

Put the goose on its carving dish and allow it to rest for about 20 minutes in a warm place before serving. Pour off the fat from the roasting pan through a sieve into a large bowl and let it cool before storing in the fridge. Deglaze the roasting pan with whatever drink you are having to accompany the goose – either cider or red wine – to make a thin gravy. Use some vegetable stock or water if necessary to make sufficient. Add salt and pepper as required and the apple jelly.

Serve the goose with a spoonful of the fluffy apples from the cavity. The roast potatoes and lightly steamed savoy cabbage are really all you need to have with such a rich meat.

STUFFING FOR GOOSE

I have used this stuffing recipe for years, as it is so fresh tasting and light with the herbs and lemon, perfect for a rich bird like goose. I think this was originally based upon an Elizabeth David recipe.

This stuffing is also lovely with roast chicken, but quarter the quantities and add some melted butter as chicken is drier than the fatty goose.

RAISED CHICKEN AND PORK PIE

I do like pies very much, and I don't think you can better a good butcher's pork pie, raised on a wooden mold, with its golden glaze. These are not bright pink inside, more like cooked meat speckled with white fat, and seasoned with lots of pepper and sage. Occasionally I make a raised pie in a hinged decorative pie mold, but you can also make individual pies molded around a jam jar. Making a hot-water crust pastry is actually very simple – like handling warm modeling clay. You just have to work fast, that's all.

It is traditional in a conventional pork pie to pour hot stock through a tiny funnel into the hole in the lid to fill the gap caused by the shrinkage of the cooked meat. The stock cools into a savory jelly. In practice I find that the juices in the meat bubble out and that there is little space for stock.

For the filling
1 medium-sized chicken, about 3 ½ lbs
8 oz pork loin chop with the fat left on
8 oz pork fillet
8 oz finely sliced bacon
Sea salt and pepper
Freshly grated nutmeg
12 large fresh sage leaves, finely chopped
3 tablespoons cider brandy
2 bunches of fresh parsley, finely chopped
For the hot-water crust pastry
12 oz goose fat (or lard)
1 cup boiling water
2 lbs unbleached plain flour
Sea salt
Beaten egg for glazing
Makes 1 large pie or 6 small ones
Oven temperature: 375°F

Strip the meat off the chicken and cut neatly into generous slices. Roughly chop the pork and bacon together, discarding any rind or bone. Don't use the food processor –

you don't want to lose the texture. Season generously with salt, pepper, nutmeg and sage, and mix in the cider brandy.

To make the pastry, add the fat to the water and boil together in a small pan. Put the flour and salt into the food processor and tip the hot liquid in while the machine is running, to form a workable dough. When it is cool enough to handle, but still very warm, cut off a quarter for the lid and keep that warm. Pat the remainder between the palms of your hands to flatten it – it should begin to look and feel rather like a warm chamois leather – and then line a large oval pie mold, 10 x 6 inches, starting at the bottom and drawing the dough up the sides so that it hangs over the edge of the mold. Work quickly, as the dough will be less pliable if it gets too cool. Roll out the remaining piece of dough to roughly the right shape for the top.

Cover the bottom of the pie with a layer of chicken, then spread some pork mixture over this followed by a thin layer of parsley. Repeat the layers until the pie is full. Put the lid over the pie, and pinch together the edges of the sides and top, sealing them together with beaten egg. Make a central hole in the lid and decorate with any leftover pieces of pastry – in braids, leaves or whatever shape takes your fancy. Cover the pie with two layers of waxed paper to protect the pastry during the long baking. Bake it for 2 hours in the preheated oven, checking from time to time that it is not overbrowning.

Take the pie out of the oven and remove the mold. Glaze the sides and top with beaten egg and return to the oven. Cook for 10 minutes to color the pastry.

To make small pies, divide the pastry into six; remove a quarter from each portion for the lid as you make each pie. Mold the warm dough around greased and well-floured jam jars. Wrap around with several layers of nonstick baking parchment or greased waxed paper, cut to the height of the pie, and tie loosely with string. Slide the pastry cases off the jars carefully, so that they don't collapse. Proceed as for the large pie, except reduce the cooking time to 1 hour. I love the way these look at every stage.

Allow to cool for several hours, preferably overnight. Cut the large pie into slices carefully, as the pastry may crumble. You get a beautiful pink, cream and green marbling effect from the layers of meat and parsley. Serve with chutney, mustard and a simple salad. What is good is that this can be cooked in advance and looks impressive. It is the sort of dish that the eighteenth-century diarist Parson Woodford describes.

GLAZED BAKED HAM

Christmas is one of the few times of year that one can justify a whole ham. It always gets eaten, and it looks and feels like part of a feast. I like ham on the bone, but I can't cook it myself so I order it from the butcher ready-cooked and simply glaze it. Don't leave it in the oven too long with the glaze or you will overcook the meat and it will lose its texture and become dry and stringy. You may prefer to have the ham boned so that it is easier to slice.

4 tablespoons clear honey
2 tablespoons Dijon mustard
1 teaspoon English mustard powder
Juice of 1 fresh orange
1 cooked ham, about 9 lbs
Serves many
Oven temperature: 450°F

Mix the honey, mustards and orange juice, and warm over a low heat to melt the honey. Cut the skin off the ham if your butcher has left it on, and score the surface of the ham fat into a diamond pattern. Do not cut so deeply that you penetrate the meat. Brush the glaze generously over the ham. Bake in the preheated oven for about 10 minutes until the glaze has slightly caramelized, watching it closely to make sure it does not overcook. Leave to cool.

JANUARY

IT IS REMARKABLE HOW we turn a corner with the New Year. The weather stays the same, daylight lengthens imperceptibly and everything is changed. In horticultural terms it is not a new year but the middle of the winter season, from which things can only get better for the gardener.

The weather, of course, controls almost everything. Statistically, this is the month when we are most likely to get snow or ice, but in recent years both of these have been rare exceptions to a very wet rule. Inevitably, the previous few months will have been cold and wet, too, so mild weather in January, in our part of the world, is bad news. The soil is turned to mud, the grass paths are a slimy quagmire and there is very little that you can do that does not create more problems than it solves.

Between the New Year and mid-April, sowing and planting dates here are not calendar-critical and might vary by as much as six weeks from one year to the next. The only yardstick to go by is the state of the soil. If it can be raked fine, is reasonably warm to touch and dry enough to walk on without sticking to your boots in lumps, then the time is right to put these very early crops into the ground, regardless of whether it is January, February or March. In the individual small beds in the vegetable garden, where we have added tons of manure and mushroom compost over the past years, the ground remains workable, and if we get a clear week we plant out the first onion sets and more garlic, and sow some early peas and more broad beans.

The rhubarb starts to grow in January, so now is the time to cover a couple of plants to force some stems to grow fast for an early picking at the end of February.

If we get a frosty spell, we try to use it to cart manure to the beds and to do pruning and tidying jobs.

WINTER PRUNING

The winter pruning of the fruit trees is a job I always look forward to. As our orchard is still very young, there is not a great deal to do other than clear any crossing branches and trim off low-growing side shoots. But even this is a pleasure. You are giving each tree absolute attention, building a balanced framework of branches so that the aesthetic pleasures of looking at it and the requirements for producing a big, healthy crop are weighed together. There are two great things to remember about pruning young trees. The first is that pruning stimulates growth rather than restricts it, and the second is that trees grow from the tips of their shoots outward. Hardly revolutionary stuff, but there is a temptation to imagine that the young tree before you is a miniature version of the mature plant that will simply swell and elevate itself upward and outward without changing its existing shape. You have to keep reminding yourself that this year's pencil-thick shoot is next year's branch and that the seemingly vulnerable central stem is the robust trunk of 10 years' time. Once you have this firmly in mind, you can prune confidently, knowing that each cut is channeling energy into the coming year's growth.

It does not matter how cold the weather is when you prune, as frost will not affect fresh wounds any more than the rest of the tree, and it is a job best done on a cold, dry day, when the ground is too hard to work. In a young orchard like ours, fruit production is less of a concern than the establishment of a framework of strong, well-spaced horizontal branches on the growing tree.

Most apples and pears fruit on spurs that have developed the previous year. These look like knobbly side shoots growing horizontally from the branches. To get the most fruit, the spurs have to be pruned back to about 4 inches each. However, some apples, such as 'Worcester Pearmain', are tip bearers, which means that the buds and fruit develop at the tips of the previous summer's growth. These need pruning less hard, reducing the leader of each branch by about one-third and cutting back any laterals to about five or six buds.

Always use sharp tools to avoid crushing or twisting branches and do not paint any cuts, as this merely seals in any damp or disease. Leave a clean cut without any ragged edges, angled down and away from the stem, and let the tree slowly heal itself.

We are growing standards, which means that the trunks have 6 feet of clear growth without any branches. The advantages of this are that they make large, beautiful trees with a canopy growing above head height, so you can walk below them and the grass can get enough light to grow right up to the trunks, and they will, in time, produce an enormous crop of fruit. But best of all, a collection of standard fruit trees makes a proper orchard, which if you are fortunate enough to have the space is a wonderful addition to a garden. An orchard is a place with an atmosphere and environment of its own. It seems to me that making places is what gardening is really about and the means that you use, with plants, hard materials or open spaces, should always be directed toward this end of creating somewhere with its own definable identity that was not there before.

CABBAGES

The cabbage crop comes into its own in January. Cabbages have a bad press here in Britain, where they are associated with a soggy, overcooked mass of lukewarm leaves. Not good. But a savoy cabbage, cut minutes before cooking,

quartered and quickly boiled or steamed so that the outer leaves are tender and the inner ones still crisp, and served simply with freshly ground pepper and very salty organic butter, is delicious. The black Tuscan kale, cavolo nero, that grows like a mini palm tree, will take more robust boiling without losing color or texture and is wonderfully tasty with pasta, roast meat or in soup.

Cabbages can look good, too. Planted in blocks they can set up a rhythm of color ranging from a zinging xanthic green as vibrant as an April euphorbia via the dark, dark green of cavolo nero, through a powdery, steely blue to the rich purple leaves of red cabbage. They can and should be beautiful.

It would take the most dedicated brassicophile to fill their winter garden with cabbages but from the range available it is surely worth growing one or two kinds that can provide the best possible ingredient to remind you that cabbage is delicious.

And they are simple enough to grow. Although summer cabbages such as 'Greyhound' are appreciably faster maturing than their winter counterparts such as 'January King' or savoys, all cabbages need quite a long growing

season, a factor that needs some planning to fit them into the garden scheme of things but is of great virtue in winter, as it carries the corollary that they stand ready for eating all winter if need be. Brassicas – the family that all types of cabbage belong to, as do cauliflowers, radishes, rutabagas, turnips and kohlrabi – all share the same preference for well-drained, well-manured soil in an open position. The manure should not be fresh, nor the site recently dug, so it is usual to grow cabbages on a piece of ground that was previously used for legumes and onions, which should have been freshly manured before they were sown and which will have left nitrogen in the soil via the nodules in the legume roots. Peas and broad beans tend to get cleared in mid- to late summer, which is when winter cabbages are planted out.

About six weeks before planting out, the cabbages are grown from seed into individual, strong plants. The traditional way is to sow them outside in a seedbed, thinning them as they grow to allow space for the plants to become bushy and robust. This is easy on space and labor, and has the advantage of not disturbing the roots more than once. However, I have more success sowing the seeds in seed trays and transplanting them into individual pots or plugs, which involves more labor but makes it much easier to protect the seedlings against slug damage and is less wasteful on seed.

Before planting out, the soil should be packed firm – as though preparing a lawn – before raking over. The cabbage head makes the plant very top-heavy so the roots, which are strong enough to grow through the compaction, must be anchored as firmly as possible. If you plant out the seedlings in blocks at 18 inch spacings, they soon cover the ground. This makes smaller cabbages than a more conventional spacing of 2 feet but looks better and stops weeds.

The soft growth of young plants is easy meat for slugs but they soon get too tough for them if they are healthy plants. But there are some more virulent potential disasters waiting for every cabbage, however tough. The first is likely to happen just after planting out and comes in the pretty, shaky flutter of the cabbage white butterfly, which has been particularly awful in recent years. In fact, there are two species of butterfly that do the damage, the large white and the small white. The large white lays its eggs on the leaves, which their yellow and black caterpillars cover by the hundred, stripping the young plants to skeletons. We pick them off by hand but I have just read that spraying with salt water works well. I wish I had known that last August. The small white lays its eggs at the base of the plants and its green caterpillars do their dastardly work less conspicuously but to just as noxious an effect.

But plants can recover from attack, so do not despair if your carefully nurtured plant is reduced to shreds almost overnight. It might yet provide a meal in a few months' time. The best thing to do to avoid the cabbage white is to put a fine net over the cabbage plants as soon as they are planted out – and over the seedbed, too, if you have sown seed outside – so that the butterfly never gets a chance to lay its eggs on them.

Clubroot is always pronounced as the worst that can happen to a cabbage (other than being cooked at a rolling boil for 20 minutes) but I have yet to experience it. It is a fungal disease that swells and misshapes the roots and, in consequence, the plants limp along in a pointless fashion. The fungus stays in the soil after the affected plants are removed, so it is important never to grow cabbages on the same site in consecutive years, and the normal advice is to have all brassicas as part of a three- or four-year rotation with legumes, root crops and onions. Like all fungi, it does best in badly ventilated, badly drained conditions and is also more prevalent in acidic soil, which is why you are often advised to lime the ground before planting cabbages.

Cabbage stalks can be slow to compost. But crush them first (and some shredders do this very well) and they will rot down at the same time as any other component of a compost heap.

STUFFED CABBAGE

This is peasant comfort food for a wintry day. Use almost any kind of cabbage – the dark savoy-type cabbages keep their color well.

1 large or 2 smaller cabbages

4 oz back bacon, all the fat removed and then chopped

8 oz mushrooms, chopped

8 oz fresh bread crumbs

3 eggs

2 tablespoons chopped fresh parsley

1 tablespoon chopped fresh chives

Sea salt and pepper

2 cups stock

Fresh thyme, marjoram and bay leaf

Fresh Tomato Sauce (see page 56) for serving

Serves 6

Put the cabbage(s) in a large pan of salted cold water and bring to a boil. Cover and simmer until the cabbage is tender – approximately 5 minutes at a boil. It will be a little underdone in the middle. Drain, stand on its base and gently pull the leaves apart so that you can cut out the heart. Leave several layers of leaves on the outside.

Quickly fry the bacon. Make the stuffing by mixing together the bacon, mushrooms, bread crumbs, eggs and herbs with the chopped cabbage heart. Season with salt and pepper. Press inside the cabbage(s) and tie them with parcel string. Braise in the stock, covered, for 35 minutes, adding thyme, bay leaf and marjoram to intensify the flavor of the stock.

Remove the string. Cut the cabbage(s) into wedges to serve, with tomato sauce thinned with some of the cooking stock. Carrots and leeks can be cooked in the stock if you want extra vegetables.

CAVOLO NERO SALAD WITH WARM CHILI
DRESSING

This delicious dressing makes winter vegetables extraordinary.

1 lb cavolo nero

2 fat cloves garlic, finely chopped

2 tablespoons olive oil

1 fresh red chili, deseeded and finely chopped, or
   ½ teaspoon dried chili flakes

Sea salt

Extra-virgin olive oil for serving

Serves 6

Wash the leaves of the cavolo nero well and strip out the midrib. Chop the leaves into two or three pieces, and blanch in salted boiling water for about 5 minutes.

Meanwhile, cook the garlic gently in the oil; do not allow it to brown. Add the chili and cook for about 1 more minute.

Drain the cavolo nero well. Add to the pan with the chili and garlic and stir. Add salt if necessary. Put into a serving bowl and add some extra-virgin olive oil. This can be eaten on its own, or with simple food such as grilled meat or fish.

CAVOLO NERO AND GARLIC CREAM SAUCE

This is good with fresh pasta made with the same recipe as the ravioli on page 71, cut into ribbons, or with a good-quality dried pasta made with eggs, such as pappardelle. This is one of the few ways to get the children to eat their greens.

1 lb cavolo nero
6 plump cloves mild garlic
1 cup heavy cream
1 tablespoon extra-virgin olive oil
2 oz Parmesan cheese, freshly grated, plus extra for serving
Sea salt and pepper
Serves 6

Strip out the midrib of the cavolo nero and discard it. Blanch the leaves in boiling salted water for approximately 5 minutes. Drain well.

Peel the garlic cloves and prick them with a fork but leave them whole. Put the garlic cloves in a pan with the cream and bring to a boil, then simmer for 10 minutes. If you want a mild sauce remove the cloves. I leave them in.

Put the cavolo nero and the cream mixture in the food processor and blend until you have a pale green sauce flecked with dark green. Return it to the pan to warm through. Add the olive oil, Parmesan and seasoning.

Mix the cooked pasta into the sauce to coat it well, and serve with extra Parmesan to sprinkle over. This makes a very quick and easy meal, and can replace pesto in winter.

CHICKEN STOCK

I never throw away a chicken carcass without making stock from it. Always make use of leftover roast chicken to make a well-flavored golden stock. A light stock can be made with an uncooked chicken if you are using the meat for another recipe (for example, the chicken and pork pie on page 104). One of the most memorable risottos I ever had was made with six chickens – only the breast meat was removed from them for the risotto and the rest was used to make an intensely flavored stock.

Stock will keep for only a couple of days in the fridge. If you are not going to use it immediately, freeze it.

Bones and trimmings from the chicken
3 cups water
1 medium-sized onion studded with 3 cloves
1 large carrot
1 large stick celery
2 bay leaves
1 teaspoon whole peppercorns
Parsley stalks
Sea salt
Makes about 3/4 pint

Put the bones and trimmings into a saucepan with the rest of the stock ingredients, except the salt, and bring to a boil, then simmer until reduced by half (about 2 hours). Strain and season well.

SAVORY PASTRY

1 lb organic unbleached plain flour
Pinch of sea salt
8 oz unsalted butter
6 tablespoons cold water

Sift the flour and put in the bowl of a food processor with the salt. Add the butter cut into small cubes. Process until the texture of bread crumbs. Add water a spoonful at a time until the mixture becomes a dough. Remove the dough, wrap in plastic wrap and rest in the fridge for 1 hour.

ONION TART

I prefer to make this as a big flat open tart that can be cut into squares, but it can be made into little individual tarts if you are feeling fancy. I rarely use beans when baking an unfilled crust – I just prick all over the bottom of the pastry crust with a fork. Although the tart is incredibly simple, you do need to take care for it to turn out well.

$\frac{1}{2}$ recipe Savory Pastry (see above)
2 lbs onions
2 oz butter
Sea salt and pepper
Sprigs of fresh thyme
Serves 6–10
Oven temperature: 375°F

Roll the pastry dough out very thinly, and line a baking tray 16 x 12 inches. Prick well, then bake unfilled in the preheated oven until pale gold.

Slice the onions as finely as possible. Melt the butter in a large saucepan or deep frying pan, add the onions and season. Cook the onions as slowly as possible, stirring occasionally, until they are soft and sweet and starting to brown slightly. This will take at least 30 minutes. If the onions start to look dry at any point add some more butter.

Spread the onions over the pastry and return to the oven to warm through. Strip the leaves from sprigs of thyme and sprinkle over the surface before serving warm. This is either a light meal with a green salad or a starter.

ROAST ONIONS

Roasting onions transforms a basic vegetable into a meltingly sweet, comforting dish. We used to eat this when we lived on the Yorkshire moors and were penniless.

Medium white onions, in their skins, 1 per person
Butter
Sea salt and pepper
Oven temperature: 450°F

Peel the onions back to a clean outer skin. Place them on a roasting dish in the preheated oven and roast until soft – approximately 1 hour. Split open, and top each with a pat of butter, sea salt and black pepper.

MONTY'S BREAD

We make bread all the year round, but somehow it seems to be more of a winter activity. Maybe it is just colder and we eat more of it. Anyway, whatever the time of year, the procedure is the same. As a rule I make very few variations on this basic loaf, which I bake once a week in the bread oven, making four or five large loaves in each batch. Breadmaking is not an exact science. Every loaf varies and every breadmaking session has a different feel to it, dependent on mood, weather and time. It is very similar to gardening in many ways, and there is something very personal about it. Consequently bread reflects the personality of the baker just as much as a garden does of the gardener. As I am not a professional cook I feel under no obligation to give you a foolproof method, but for the record, this is how I do my own baking. This is not a recipe for "quick" bread,

but can spread over two days, although it probably only uses a couple of hours of my time in that period. It may seem long-winded and complicated, but is essentially very simple, mixing flour, yeast and water and letting them work with each other to make a "bakable" dough.

I use active dry yeast (to paraphrase Elizabeth David, it wouldn't be much use if it was not active), which I buy in a can. Once opened this keeps perfectly well in the warmest part of the fridge. The flour I use is white, organic, unbleached, "strong breadmaking flour" that I buy in sacks. The fact that it is strong means that it has a high gluten content and therefore takes a little more working and a little longer to rise than many flours.

I always use a starter based upon the Italian *biga*. This is a dough made with very little yeast; it can be stored for up to a week in the fridge. It stimulates the main dough to work better, and adds a chewy texture and much better flavor to the baked bread. You could – and probably should – keep a golf-ball-sized lump from each batch of dough to be the starter for the next batch, but I usually forget and have to make my starter anew each time.

3 ½ teaspoons dry yeast
8–10 cups of warm water
5 ½ lbs unbleached strong white flour
2 tablespoons fine sea salt
Oven temperature: 450°F
(then) 375°F
Makes 4 or 5 loaves

I dissolve 1 teaspoon of the yeast in a cup of warm water and leave it on the Aga or in a similar warm place for at least 10 minutes. Leaving the yeast to work does no harm and it can be left for a couple of hours, which will improve the texture of the bread.

Put the yeast into a large mixing bowl, add another cup of lukewarm water and stir it up. Slowly add enough flour until you have a very sticky, wet dough. As a rough guide,

you will need about 4 cups of flour, but you should go based on the dough rather than any finite quantities. Stir it for up to 10 minutes with a wooden spoon, turning it over on itself. This is hard work. The starter dough is very elastic and sticky and does not easily stir. Keep at it as this will improve the texture and quality of the final loaf. Alternatively, you could use an electric mixer.

Turn the starter dough out into another large bowl that you have oiled and cover with plastic wrap or a damp cloth. Leave it in a warmish place (i.e., not cold) for at least 24 hours to rise. It will double in size in the first 3 hours, so make sure that the bowl is large enough to accommodate this.

Put the bowl in the fridge overnight and take it out again in the morning at least 3 hours before you intend to use the starter. If you are not using it that day, leave it out for the day and then put it back into the fridge until you need it. The longer you keep it the sourer it becomes. You can use this starter in two ways – either, as I tend to, in its entirety to make up a batch of loaves, or spread over a number of different bakings.

Our main loaf is not English at all, but based upon the Pane Pugliese of Italy. The most perfect loaf of this type that I have eaten was sold in a supermarket in Lagos in southern Portugal, so I guess that I am after an archetypal loaf rather than a specific recipe. Whatever its origin, it should be a large, round loaf with a deep crust and a chewy interior, pocked with large holes.

I mix the remaining 2 ½ teaspoons of dry yeast with a cup of warm water, give it a good stir and let it sort itself out. Again, nothing is lost if you let this happen slowly over a couple of hours. Then I pour it into a very large mixing bowl, add the remaining 6 cups of water, the salt and at least half the starter dough – no need to be exact about that. I mix this up until the starter dough is thoroughly mixed. It is very squishy and takes a little while.

Then I add about 4 ½ lbs of flour, a cup at a time, mixing it like I did the starter. The final dough is very wet and sticky, so do not be tempted to add too much flour. A good guide is that if you can handle it and knead it, then it is too dry. It should stick to the side of the bowl when pulled away and be very elastic.

Turn it into another large bowl (I use our jam-making saucepan) that you have oiled, cover and put in a warm place for 3 hours. It will at least double in size in that time. I have done a great deal of experimentation with this stage of the rising and have found that it does best with real warmth – which is difficult to find in our drafty old house. An airing cupboard is best. The time is not critical, but with this bread it is always better to leave everything for too long rather than too short a time.

Tip the dough on to a very well-floured table. I then divide it into the number of loaves I want to make. Ideally the loaves should be as big as possible, but the size of your oven door will dictate that. Each lump of wet dough should be flattened with the palm of your hand and then rolled with the fingers and thumbs toward you. Turn it 90 degrees, flatten it again (you will notice that it feels much tighter and less elastic this time) and roll it up again. Shape it into a round so that the top is taut. Scrape it off the table and put it onto a board for the next rise.

This process is messy and sticky, hence have all the flour that you will need at hand. There are two utensils that are invaluable for this stage: a dough scraper and silicone cooking liners. The dough scraper cuts, lifts and moves the wet dough and the cooking liner is reusable, utterly nonstick or unburnable, can be picked up with the dough on it, and the dough stays on it until it has cooked enough to be handled.

When you have prepared each loaf, sprinkle the tops with flour and cover them with a tea towel before putting them back in your warm place to rise again. They will need at least an hour; I find that nearer 2 hours is better.

The bread oven is lit just before this final rise, as it takes 2 hours to heat and prepare. A fire is lit inside the oven with paper and dry sticks and then, when it is going, a bundle of very dry sticks is put in. Invariably smoke fills the house and there is much coughing, peering in to see how it is doing, and opening and shutting of doors to get the draft right. It is great fun, but a gas or electric oven would do perfectly well with no preparation at all. Occasionally I use our stove, and I am sure that I would not be able to tell the difference between the bread oven and the Aga.

Whatever you use must be hot initially and be able to be turned down (or cool down) after about 15–20 minutes. The Aga has two hot ovens, so we move the bread from one to the other for the second, cooler stage of the baking. A couple of quarry tiles put in the oven half an hour before baking will replicate the brick floor of the bread oven pretty well.

Slash the top of each loaf in a crisscross fashion before putting it on the silicone liner. The cuts are important, as they enable the loaf to expand upward rather than sideways in the oven, and so improve the texture a lot. Bake the loaves in the preheated hot oven for 15 minutes before checking that the crust is firm enough to handle. Then change the position of the loaves to ensure they bake evenly. Turn the oven down and bake them for a further 30 minutes. To test if the loaves are cooked, tap the base to see if they sound hollow.

When they are done, let them cool completely on a wire rack before eating. We always have one loaf in the bread bin, one in the fridge wrapped in a polythene bag and the rest in polythene bags in the freezer. The bread is always slightly drier after defrosting, but this is a moist, chewy loaf so, short of baking every other day, freezing is an acceptable compromise.

FEBRUARY

IN THIS GARDEN February has a deadline. February 15 is Sarah's birthday, and that is the date by which we try to have all our seeds ordered so that we can start sowing the first seeds in seed trays and in the greenhouse borders. In a way, this is the start of our new year. The days are longer – if still frustratingly short. The snowdrops, hellebores and crocuses are all out, and often the primroses, too – my favorite flower of all. Buds are swelling on the roses and if the weather is mild there are signs of life in the herbaceous border. It does not matter that the weather is often appalling because there is the tangible promise of a better time. So, by the middle of February, there is a surge of energy and hope running through the garden. The quality of light measurably changes, too, becoming yellower and warmer daily, albeit often just for a few precious moments at a time.

We always lay all the seeds out on the kitchen table and place them in groups. There is a pleasing symmetry here with the journey of these plants starting and ending in the kitchen. All the salad crops go together, the beans line up with the knobbly packets of peas, the root vegetables have their patch, as do all the herbs and the greenhouse crops such as tomatoes, cucumbers, peppers and so on. Physical, graphical order is laid out like armies on a plain. The seeds are then batched up in a temporal pattern, allowing for germinating conditions and successional sowings. They are then bundled into a box and, as often as not, completely muddled up in the process. But this does not matter, because the laying out of the seeds has linked all the paper packets to the garden and real, edible plants rather than a series of lists and plans on paper. It is a sign that the

the garden itself. You can only enjoy the background stuff as an end in itself – and this is where I fail.

In the potting shed all the seed trays and pots will have been scrubbed and stacked by now, a good supply of organic, peat-free compost delivered, together with perlite and vermiculite. From now on, the seeds live in the potting shed and if the weather is bad there is always work to do in there. But all energy is focused on work outside. February is the last chance to plant any deciduous trees, hedges or shrubs before the roots begin to grow. The combination of daylight, dry ground, dry weather and the free time to work in the garden is a rare one at this time of year, so any opportunity to get out and plant is snatched.

This has to compete with work on paths, which is a constant project here as we are slowly trying to convert all the paths that take working traffic from grass to a hard surface. This is a very big job. It involves removing the turf (which gets stacked face to face in a large block and, after a couple of years, becomes perfect for making seed-starting medium), digging out the topsoil to a depth of 18 inches – the topsoil having to be wheeled away and spread elsewhere in the garden – putting in 9 inches of hardcore topped with 3–4 inches of crushed rock to ensure good drainage, then laying the brick or stone path on a layer of sand. We hack out these paths painfully slowly, foot by foot over the years, knowing that there is no other way of gaining access to the soil during the winter months. Because of the maintenance work that growing plants require, work on the paths can only be done in winter, and February is the end of this period.

But seed sowing can take place after dark. This feels like stealing time and is a treat, knowing that you are not

engagement with the garden is real and direct and marks the end of weeks of planning. For much of the winter the garden sulks outside. It is a lumpen thing like a chicken in molt or a catwalk model in curlers and zits. The thing itself is still there but not, certainly not, at its best. I find it hard to engage with it. Disciplined effort is required to order seeds and compost, and to do all the preparatory things that gardens require. I like my engagement to be direct and with

Above Filling a seed tray with seed-starting medium mixed with extra perlite. The high sides to the workbench keep the medium in place without getting in the way of any seed sowing, transplanting or potting up. *Opposite* A healthy basil seedling being transplanted or, as we British say, "pricked out." Holding the seedling by a leaf minimizes any damage to the delicate roots.

constrained by time or weather, working in the cozy potting shed listening to the radio and gradually accumulating plant material for the coming season.

If there has not been an opportunity at the end of January, it is good to get all the onion sets planted before the end of February. 'Turbo' and 'Sturon' are both reliably good and store well. By putting them in the ground in February, they have a chance to develop to a decent size before harvest. The crucial factor for onions is to keep them weed free throughout the growing period, as they react badly to competition for moisture and nutrition.

PARSLEY

You can eat leeks almost all the year round – which is why they have for so long been a staple of the homegrown diet — and with a little organization you can do the same with parsley. But it comes into its own in February, not because it is at its best, but because it is still good at a time when there is not much else. Parsley is wonderful stuff, spanning the tenuous divide between vegetables and herbs. We grow it in the vegetable garden, just as we do garlic and basil, and treat all three as annual crops.

I have often heard people complain about the difficulties of getting parsley to germinate, but this is not a problem I have experienced. It likes rich, well-drained ground that never dries out, and we always sow it directly where it is to grow. It does need warm soil, and the best judge of that is to use your hands. If the ground has any chill to it at all, wait a while for it to warm up.

Parsley has long taproots and does not transplant at all well, so thin the plants ruthlessly *in situ*, leaving 6 inches between each one. This will seem excessive when you do it, but will make all the difference to the longevity of the crop, as each plant will then get maximum moisture and nutrition. We only grow flat-leaf parsley, because it has a better taste and better texture for cooking. Curly or moss-leaf parsley is only any use as a garnish, and a garnish is no good to anyone at all.

Parsley is a biennial, so will go to seed in its second growing season. Once it does this, the leaves become fewer and much coarser and are of no use to the cook. This makes it important to time your sowings carefully so that you get the maximum use from the crop.

In my experience, a sowing in mid- to late April will provide pickings from July through to the following December, when it will go to seed and should be dug up. A second sowing in June will provide a good crop from September to May, and a third in August will germinate before autumn and overwinter as small seedlings that will grow and provide pickings from May onward. There might be a bit of a lag in April and May between the demise of one sowing and the decent growth of the next, but plant covers put over the August-sown crop in February will help to avert that. I also find that if you cut each plant to the ground as it goes to seed, water it well and cover it, it produces another picking of small, fresh leaves before going to seed again.

LEEKS

The member of the allium family that has looked good all winter, and that is invaluable when there is little else to harvest, is the leek. Leeks were a fixture of the medieval diet and are certain to have been grown and eaten from this garden for at least the last 1,000 years.

We plant out a batch of seedlings in July to develop slowly and become ready for harvest in the new year. Like parsnips, leeks store perfectly well in the ground, to be dug as and when you need them, and they can stay there until it is required for something else. One year I left a block of leeks all summer and they developed the most wonderful flower heads – just like agapanthus with curling, sinuous stems. Wonderful!

I always sow leeks in a seed tray in the greenhouse, between February and May, looking to get as many as half a dozen different batches to give a succession of harvestable leeks rather than one huge glut. They can also be sown in a seedbed outside, or even directly where they are to grow, but need a temperature of at least 45°F to germinate.

I transplant them into pots when they are about ¼ inch or so thick. I have no absolute yardstick to know when to do this – just as soon as you think you can is perhaps the best rule. They have long, delicate roots, so this operation has to be done very carefully. Water them well and grow them on in a cold frame or in a sheltered position outside until they are about the thickness of a skewer or 5 inch nail. As with all members of the allium family, the ground that they are to grow in must be deeply dug and well manured if you are to get the best from the crop. The one really important factor is good drainage – which thorough digging and the addition of plenty of organic material should deal with, however heavy your ground is.

Make holes with a dibber about 6 inches apart (the closer they are spaced the thinner the leeks will be) and about 3–4 inches deep, and pop a leek seedling into each one. It does not matter if they all but disappear down the holes: better that they are in too deep than too shallow. Fill the holes with water, not soil. The water will be sufficient to secure the roots into the ground. (Although you may find that a bird tweaks at the odd one, pulling it up, just put it back in again.) As the leeks grow, they will fill the holes and have a chance to expand properly.

They are a remarkably undemanding crop; just hoe between them weekly and water them in dry weather. As spring progresses, the occasional leek will develop a strong central, flowering stem. Cut this off and use the leek as soon as possible.

BROCCOLI

In the vegetable garden the broccoli starts to come into flower and the first picking is usually at the beginning of the month. This is a high point in the culinary year for us. I rate purple sprouting broccoli as highly as asparagus, as one of the great seasonal treats of the year. It takes a long time to bear fruit but, when it does, it is delicious and well worth

the wait, and because it grows predominantly through the winter months it does not occupy space that would otherwise be more productive.

Although the leaves can be eaten, it is the immature flower heads that broccoli is grown for. These look like mini cauliflowers on stalks that, if unpicked, will develop into yellow flowers. Broccoli is sown in May or June in a seedbed along with the cabbages and treated in exactly the same way, except perhaps thinning it to a wider spacing – to as much as 6 inches – because the plants grow tall and heavy and therefore need room to develop strongly.

There is no need to plant out the seedlings before late August, so I find that it makes a good crop to follow on after French beans. Plant them at least 2 feet apart in blocks, putting them deeply into well-firmed soil. In my experience it is better to put in stakes when you plant, and tie them up a couple of times as they grow. Unstaked broccoli has a habit of drooping to the ground and then growing up again like a U-bend.

Harvest the purple flower heads as soon as they form. This will encourage them to grow more side shoots. Take the best "spears" from each plant but never strip a plant completely, as this will stop it producing any more. If you are lucky and it is a cool spring, you can go on picking until May – which is when you sow seeds to start the cycle all over again.

FRIDAY, FEBRUARY 13:
Exquisite morning – big full moon in blue sky – thrush
singing – snowdrops, hellebores and crocuses perfect.
Planted two more 'Doyenné du Comice' to complete the
pear avenue and five apples ('Worcester Pearmain',
'Hereford Beefing' and 'Tillington Court').
Planted onion sets: 75 x 'Turbo', 75 x 'Centurion F1',
75 x 'Stuttgart Giant', 50 x 'Sturon'.
Moved 25 garlic plants that are growing from bits left in
ground after last year's crop.
Extraordinary day. Best February weather ever. Hot!

PURPLE SPROUTING BROCCOLI WITH ANCHOVIES

I love this way of cooking broccoli. It is based upon the recipe from the River Café, and we have cooked it so often that it has become part of the repertoire of the household.

2 lbs purple sprouting broccoli

5 cloves garlic

3 tablespoons olive oil

Pinch of dried chili flakes or diced fresh chili to taste

6 anchovy fillets

For serving

6 slices rough country bread

1 clove garlic, halved

Extra-virgin olive oil

2 lemons

Serves 6

Trim the broccoli, leaving evenly sized stems with some leaves. Blanch in boiling salted water for 3 minutes and drain.

Roughly chop 2 cloves of garlic, and gently cook in 2 tablespoons of the olive oil until soft but not brown. Add the chili flakes. Stir in the anchovies until they have melted and amalgamated with the oil and garlic. Add the blanched broccoli and cook for no more than 5 minutes or the broccoli florets will begin to break up. In another pan, fry the remaining garlic, sliced thinly lengthwise, in the remaining tablespoon of oil until crisp and golden.

Meanwhile, toast the slices of bread on both sides. Rub with the halved clove of garlic and pour over some extra-virgin olive oil. Put the toast on a large plate, pile the broccoli on each slice and squeeze some juice from one of the lemons over each. Sprinkle over the fried garlic. Serve with wedges of lemon, as a starter or light lunch.

VENISON IN A PASTRY PUFF

The woods around here are full of deer, and alleged ex-special-forces soldiers cull them for sale. Baking in a pastry crust is particularly good for venison, which is very dry. All the meat juices are sealed in, and the butter in the pastry bastes the meat as it cooks. It does look rather odd, but when it is cooked and you break it open, the steaming aromatic meat sitting on juice-soaked pastry is spectacular. Have this hot with a sweet sauce. Slice it and give everyone a little piece of the pastry (you are supposed to throw the pastry away or give it to the hounds, but I think it is too good for that).

½ teaspoon sea salt
½ teaspoon black peppercorns
½ teaspoon juniper berries
1 boned haunch of venison, about 4 lbs
Large bunch of fresh sage (30 or more leaves)
1 recipe Savory Pastry (see page 118)
4 oz Damson Cheese (see page 57) or wild fruit jelly
Serves 8–10
Oven temperature: 375°F

Crush the salt, peppercorns and juniper berries together with a pestle and mortar. Wash and dry the meat and season with the juniper mixture. Lay the sage leaves all over the surface. Roll out the pastry dough on a floured surface in one piece. It doesn't want to be too thin – ¼ and ½ inch thick – and it should be large enough to encase the meat completely. Set the joint on the pastry and wrap it up. Join the edges of the pastry with water, pinching together to seal. Put it in a roasting dish and cover the top with lightly greased aluminium foil so that the pastry doesn't burn during the cooking. Cook in the preheated oven for about 3 hours.

Melt the Damson Cheese or jelly gently in a little pan until it is warm and runny, and serve with the meat. There will be a little juice in the roasting dish, so make use of this as a precious gravy.

RABBIT TERRINE

Although this is an effort to prepare, it can be made in advance and is enough for two meals. We eat this with rhubarb chutney, salad leaves and fresh bread.

1 oz butter
1 medium onion, finely chopped
2 cloves garlic, finely chopped
14 oz pork tenderloin
7 oz skinless belly pork
18 oz prepared rabbit, off the bone (2 rabbits)
7 oz home-cured smoked streaky bacon, sliced
5 ½ oz pork back fat
Sea salt and pepper
1 small wineglass apple brandy
1 tablespoon chopped fresh parsley
1 tablespoon chopped fresh thyme
1 dessert spoon chopped fresh sage
5 ½ oz home-cured unsmoked streaky bacon, sliced
Oven temperature: 375°F
Serves 12

Butter a 5½-cup terrine with half the butter. Melt the remaining butter and gently cook the onion and garlic without allowing them to color. Remove from the heat.

Cut up the pork tenderloin, belly pork, rabbit meat, smoked bacon (remove the rind first) and pork fat until it is quite finely textured. Mix these all together in a large bowl with seasoning, the brandy and the garlic and onion.

Pack the mixture into the terrine and spread a neat layer of unsmoked streaky bacon slices across the top. Cover with foil and set in a bain marie (or in a roasting dish with water coming halfway up the side of the dish). Bake in the preheated oven for about 1½ hours. Stick a skewer in and see if the juices run clear; if not, return to cook a little longer. Allow to cool slightly before pressing with a weight on the surface to give a dense texture. Serve cold.
Variation Use chicken breasts in place of the rabbit.

ROAST LEEKS

Roasting intensifies the flavor of leeks. Gritty leeks are very unpleasant, so it is essential to remove all the soil from them. Prepare the leeks by cutting off the roots, including $1/2$ inch of the bottom, and quite a lot of the green tops. Do this outside because it is messy; then you can put the roots and leaves straight on the compost heap.

12 medium-sized leeks
About 2 tablespoons olive oil
Sea salt and pepper
Serves 6
Oven temperature: 375°F

Carefully halve the leeks lengthwise and wash out any grit. Find a roasting pan that they will fit in neatly, head to toe. Pack them in tightly, and add a little water to cover the bottom of the tin, the olive oil, and some salt and pepper. It is very important that they don't dry out. Roast in the preheated oven for about 25 minutes – turn them halfway through so that they cook evenly. The edges may brown slightly. To finish, add a little more olive oil. The cooked leeks will be soft but not slimy. These are also good cold with a squeeze of lemon juice.

PIZZA

Pizzas cooked in the bread oven are a major performance. All the ingredients for the topping are laid out on the kitchen table, and the pizza dough is made at least 2 hours in advance and allowed to rise. The house fills with smoke, and the process can be tense, but the cooked pizza is so good – crisp floury base, with melting hot ingredients, the best we have ever tasted – that the drama seems worth it.

The traditional way to bake is to put the pizza base on the paddle ready to go into the oven, but it is probably better to put it on an oiled flat metal tray.

For the dough
4 teaspoons dry yeast
1 teaspoon sugar
2 cups warm water
2 lbs unbleached strong flour plus extra for
    kneading and rolling
4 tablespoons olive oil
2 teaspoons sea salt
For the topping (use any combination of the following)
Roasted or Fresh Tomato Sauce (see page 56)
Stewed onions (finely sliced and cooked slowly in
    olive oil until soft)
Mozzarella cheese, sliced
Artichoke hearts (cooked in olive oil until soft)
'Red Treviso' (chicory), roughly chopped
Anchovies, capers or black olives
Lots of fresh herbs – oregano, basil, thyme leaves
Tiny strips of ham
Extra olive oil
Makes at least six 10 inch pizzas
Oven temperature: 475°F

For the dough, mix the yeast and sugar into the warm water. When the yeast has dissolved, stir in half the flour. Mix in the oil and salt, then add the rest of the flour and knead on a lightly floured surface for about 10 minutes until all the flour has been absorbed and the dough is smooth and resilient. Put the dough in an oiled bowl, oil the surface gently and cover with a damp cloth. Leave to rise for a couple of hours. It should double in size.

Punch the dough down, and divide into at least six equal pieces. Roll each piece out on a well-floured surface as thinly and evenly as possible to make an approximately 10 inch round. Each person chooses their toppings and the pizza is baked in the preheated oven for approximately 8 minutes. This will vary according to the thickness of the base and the ingredients.

Punching down the dough after it has risen before taking it out of the bowl and rolling it into pizza bases. Although pizza is essentially just very thin bread baked with a flavoring spread on top, it has none of the slow mystery of bread dough and is very quick to make. We often make the dough only half an hour before baking.

Pizza is best when kept simple, and homemade pizza is one of the best of simple meals. Good homemade tomato sauce, onions gently fried in olive oil, mozzarella, lots of fresh herbs and a few anchovies is as complicated as it gets in our household. As always, the better the ingredients, the simpler the preparation can be.

MARCH

THE MOST THRILLINGLY EVOCATIVE sound of the year here in western England always comes in the first few days of March, usually as I am walking the dogs at night. It is the call of the first curlews, a long, bubbling sound, starting low and rising reedily into the dark before falling away. It is as seasonal as the daffodils and every bit as beautiful. They gather throughout March and April on the marshy water meadows that abut onto this garden, massing into dozens before mating and going elsewhere to nest. For the few months that they are with us we are blessed.

It is in March, too, that we make the first cut of grass. However predictable, the smell of the first cut of spring is always intoxicating and heart-stopping in intensity. It is happiness. The garden is an accumulation of all the experiences to be had within it, be they horticultural or not.

In some ways, this underlines my own uneasiness with the word *gardening*. It does not do justice to the range of experience that you get when working outside with the land. I recently asked a friend what single image *gardening* conjured up for him, and he replied: "The sound of two rooks as they make their way home across a fading winter sky." There speaks a gardener after my own heart.

And there is daily more outside to *be* in. Northern winters may be long and dark, but northern springs are matchless. They grow like the curlews' cry, almost painfully hopeful, fed by tiny daily increments of light and heat. Sometimes the combination of both is such that we can take our lunch outside as early as March, blinking like newly released prisoners, feeling as though we are somehow cheating winter.

There is a ritual to potato sowing. *Top left* A sprouted seed potato with ideal stubby shoots. *Bottom left* The soil must be well cultivated so a deep drill can be easily drawn through it. *Right* The seed potatoes are placed in rows 24 inches apart before covering the row over to make a ridge.

POTATOES

Seed potatoes appear for sale early in the New Year so that they might be sprouted. This involves laying them out in egg boxes, seed trays or some such container in a cool, light place that is protected from frost. Slowly, they develop sprouts. Everyone has opened a bag of potatoes in the cupboard in late winter or spring to find that they have sprouted translucent white spaghetti shoots. But what you want from seed potatoes are knobbly green sprouts, no more than 1 inch in length. The reason you sprout them is to make the growing process much faster once they are planted. This can be important in cold areas because potatoes, coming as they do from the Andes, are not hardy, so the quicker they start growing, the better the crop will be before frost comes along and kills the leaves; once the leaves are dead, the potatoes cannot grow, so they wither in size or number.

It is perfectly possible to grow potatoes from your own store-bought sprouting ones, but they will be prone to virus diseases and the crop will be bigger and much healthier if seed potatoes, which are grown in sterilized soil, are used.

Potatoes are divided into three groups: first early, second early and main crop. First earlies mature after about 100 days, second earlies between 110 and 120 days, and main crop after 130 days. All can be stored unharvested in the ground for at least a month after maturation, but first and second earlies are best lifted and eaten as soon as possible. However, first earlies in particular are tastier if left in the ground until the last possible moment before cooking, as some of their starch starts to turn to sugar within about an hour of lifting, detracting from the flavor. For this reason it is better to sow a mixture of first and second earlies to get a succession of potatoes as they are ready, rather than having to lift the whole crop at once or leave them in the ground too long.

There are over 400 different varieties of potato, yet less than 30 are commercially cultivated and the real choice commonly available is much less than that, since the vast majority of potatoes are sold in stores labeled merely as "Reds" or "Whites" – the former red skinned and often yellow fleshed like 'Desiree', and the latter yellow skinned and floury like 'King Edward'.

The best early potato is one romantically called 'BF15'. This is produced from 'Belle de Fontenay' (hence the *BF* prefix) and has a wonderfully smooth, waxy consistency while retaining the necessary lightness and softness that makes new potatoes different from any main-crop varieties (other than their much greater sweetness). 'Belle de Fontenay' is a very good second early, which is ready a week or two after 'BF15'. 'Rocket' is the earliest of all – after as little as 90 days—but is not remarkable. I shall not grow it again.

Planting is easy. All you have to do is make a hole and push them in it to produce a reasonable crop, and in the garden, reasonable is enough. However, to maximize the yield, ease of harvesting and cultivation, the ground for potatoes should be well dug and as richly manured as you can make it, preferably a few months before planting. Make a drill or shallow trench about 6 inches deep and put the potatoes in the bottom at about 12-inch spacings. The wider the spacing the bigger the potatoes, therefore new potatoes tend to be sown closer together and main crop, especially baking varieties, wider apart. Rake the soil at the sides of the drill back to make a low mound along the line of seed potatoes. Each row wants to be 24 inches apart.

Potatoes are very good for planting in new ground that you want to use later in the year, as they open up the soil and their thick top growth stops any weeds growing. Rather than dig the ground over, just make the trench and fill the bottom with compost, putting the seed potatoes directly onto that before covering them over with soil. I have grown a perfectly good crop on fresh grassland by lifting the turf along the line of each trench, placing the seed potatoes directly onto the soil and replacing the turf upside down on top of them.

Water is really important. The crucial period is between a month after planting and a month before harvest, when they must have a good soak once a week.

With anything other than a large garden, it makes sense to stick to earlies for a few delicious meals, or to grow a really special main-crop variety like 'Pink Fir Apple', 'Belle de Fontenay' or 'Rattle'. Blue varieties such as 'Edzell Blue' or 'Arran Victory' do more for the eye than the taste buds.

ROCKET AND LAND CRESS

Rocket (or arugula) became fashionable in restaurants some years ago in the same way that cavolo nero and various types of chicory have become trendy recently. I am all for these fads and fancies because they bring to public consciousness tastes that would otherwise remain largely unknown. They also set up a demand for seeds. Rocket seed can now be bought at any hardware shop or garden center, making this delicious leaf available to anyone with a scrap of soil to grow it in. And hardly anything is easier to grow. But to get the best from it you need cool (not cold) weather, rich soil and plenty of moisture, otherwise it goes to seed almost before it forms leaves.

I have tried sowing rocket almost every month of the year and now restrict it to a sowing in March and April, and again in August and September. Almost every seed will germinate, throwing up a line of green in a week or so, but thin it scrupulously to 6 inches between each plant. This wide spacing allows the plants to develop wide rosettes of leaves and to respond vigorously when cropped to the ground by growing a fresh batch of leaves. As with all salad crops, the thinnings need not be wasted, as they are delicious washed and eaten, roots and all.

Invariably, the plants will go to seed as the weather warms up. The flowers are attractive and tasty, albeit distinctly hot. They can be left until the seeds sown later in the year begin to provide a fresher alternative.

Land cress is often sown in late summer to use over winter but will also do perfectly well sown in early spring

for a quick catch crop in ground intended for French or runner beans. It is very similar in taste and habit to rocket, although it has been used as a substitute for watercress since the seventeenth century and, like watercress, it prefers damp, or even wet, conditions. We grow it exactly like rocket, as a variation on the same theme.

RHUBARB

The rhubarb is growing strongly by March and there are stems to be picked for eating fresh. It is strange stuff, half fruit and half vegetable, producing its astringent stems topped with miniature lime green leaves, which by midsummer will become great elephants' ears. Commercial rhubarb growers keep rhubarb roots only for 2 or 3 years and then discard them, but I know people who have grown the same plant for 50 years and I see no reason to regard rhubarb as anything other than a permanent fixture.

The rhubarb in this garden is all 'Timperley Early' and came as castoffs from a rhubarb farm in Yorkshire, where they had borne a crop in long, low sheds lit only by candlelight so that the stems would stay pale and grow straight. Rhubarb is extremely sensitive to light, growing as the days lengthen; traditionally, clay covers are placed over a few plants to block out the light and create a warm microclimate for an early picking of pale stems. When I was a child our old gardener always put a lump of fresh cow's manure on top of the plant cover to "draw the rhubarb up." I am sure that it did no more than seal the light out but I still do the same, willing the new shoots upward with a hat of muck!

Rhubarb roots are woody, fibrous chunks that can be planted early in the new year, with at least one bud just above the soil surface. An old plant that is predominantly producing thin stems (and what, one might ask, is wrong with that?) can be dug up in autumn after it drops its leaves and chopped into smaller pieces, with the central area of root discarded. As long as each remaining section of root has at least one bud, it can be replanted to create a new

plant. Rhubarb is much more productive if planted in a sunny site with lots of organic material dug deeply into the soil, and mulched each autumn with a thick layer of manure or compost. It is best to leave a new plant to develop strong roots, pulling stems only in its second year. The stems are best pulled or snapped off at the base rather than cut.

SUNDAY, MARCH 29:
Clocks went forward.
Drizzle all day. Warm.
Made two new sets of fences in the afternoon. Very wet and muddy. But looks good.
Sarah sowed basil and bronze fennel in seed trays.

RHUBARB CHUTNEY

Every day between 4 and 12 people sit down to lunch in our house. It is often simply bread, cheese and a chutney, such as this one.

4 lbs rhubarb
3 medium-sized red onions, finely chopped
1 oz ginger root, peeled and grated
1 ½ lbs sugar
1 tablespoon yellow raisins
1 pint red wine vinegar
Makes about six 1 lb jars

Have your jam jars ready, cleaned, sterilized and warmed in the oven so that the glass doesn't crack when you put in the hot chutney.

Wash and trim the rhubarb and remove the poisonous leaves. Chop the stalks into 1 inch lengths. Put all the ingredients into a heavy-bottomed preserving pan, and bring gently to a boil. Simmer for at least 40 minutes until the mixture has thickened and slightly reduced. Allow to cool slightly, then fill the prepared jam jars. Seal with jam pot covers (a waxed paper circle and cellophane cap).
Variation You can substitute beets and apples for rhubarb. I have made a midwinter chutney with 3 lbs of beets, boiled whole, skinned and then cut into little cubes, and 1 lb of 'Bramley's' apples, peeled and sliced, then cooked until soft in a little water. Add these two ingredients to those listed above (minus the rhubarb) and use the method previously described.

WINTER SALAD

This is prettier than a supermarket bag of mixed salad. The freshness of it is so apparent that all it needs is a simple dressing. The leaves must be dry – if you pick leaves from your garden carefully, they may need no washing at all. If you do have to wash them, use a salad spinner for drying.

It is one of the most frequently used pieces of kitchen equipment in our house. Watery lettuces symbolize dreary English salads to me.

Use a combination of rocket, radicchio and lamb's lettuce
For the dressing
3 parts extra-virgin olive oil
1 part balsamic vinegar
Sea salt

Mix the dressing ingredients together and pour over the washed and dried leaves.

RHUBARB TART

Stewed rhubarb and custard are a good combination if cooked carefully, but have all the glamor of a school dinner. The idea of this tart came from a covered market at Le Touquet, where I saw a stall selling rhubarb tarts in a golden custard. I thought it was a brilliant idea, and here is my version. You can adapt this method for any fruit that needs a little cooking – gooseberries, plums or greengages.

1 lb early young rhubarb
$^{1}/_{2}$ recipe Sweet Pastry (see left)
For the custard
$^{1}/_{2}$ vanilla pod
$^{1}/_{2}$ cup milk
$^{1}/_{3}$ cup heavy cream
3 large egg yolks
2 $^{1}/_{2}$ oz golden caster sugar or granulated sugar
1 heaping teaspoon unbleached plain flour
Serves 8
Oven temperature: 425°F

SWEET PASTRY

8 oz unsalted butter, at room temperature
4 oz vanilla caster sugar or granulated sugar
2 eggs, beaten
1 lb unbleached plain flour
Pinch of sea salt
Makes enough for at least two 10 inch tarts

In a processor, cream the butter and sugar. Add the eggs in a trickle while the machine is running. Scrape down the mixture from the sides of the bowl to make sure it is all mixed properly. Sift the flour and add the flour and salt, a spoonful at a time, as it is being processed. This makes a very stiff dough.

Wrap it in plastic wrap and rest for at least 2 hours in the fridge. It can be kept in the fridge for several days (remove from the fridge 15 minutes before use).

Discard the leaves and wash the rhubarb stalks. Cut into 1 inch lengths.

Line a 12 inch baking tin with the pastry, but do not trim the edges. Prick well, then bake unfilled for about 10 minutes until slightly colored. The reason to leave the crust untrimmed is that you are going to cook this twice, and the edges are vulnerable to blackening. You carefully trim it after it comes out of the oven for the final time.

Infuse the vanilla pod in the warmed milk and cream for about 20 minutes. Remove the pod, split it open lengthwise and scrape out the dark seeds. Return the seeds to the milk and cream. Add the egg yolks, sugar and flour and whisk together, or you can use a food processor. Pour the custard into the pastry shell, arrange the rhubarb pieces over it, and bake for about 20–25 minutes. Serve warm.

Variation Instead of using rhubarb, thinly slice one blood orange and place the slices all over the custard.

Blood Orange Tart This is made with the same recipe as the Rhubarb Tart (see opposite) but substituting blood oranges for the rhubarb. The oranges are finely sliced with the peel left on, giving a bitter marmalade flavor that cuts through the richness of the custard.

APRIL

APRIL IS A SCHIZOPHRENIC MONTH for the kitchen gardener. On the one hand, spring is roaring in, everything is growing and the days are lengthening. It is probably the busiest time of the year, when we are catching up, finishing everything that was not possible in winter and getting as much in the ground and sown indoors as possible.

But on the other hand, the supply of fresh food is diminishing all the time. There is no fruit at all and there has not been for three months, nor will there be until the first cherries in May. The vegetables that successfully overwintered are either finished or struggling not to go to seed. If it is a cold, wet spring – and England has been known to have very cold, very wet springs – then the herbs will be showing very reluctantly. There is a real chance of night frosts at any time in the month but this high pressure will be matched by as many days of hot sun. Best of all, for the gardener, are soft days – showery, uncertain, but mild and inviting growth by the hour.

Whatever the weather, the blossoms will be erupting in a pink and white froth throughout the month, providing plenty of food for the soul. Herefordshire has more standard fruit trees and better blossoms than anywhere else in the UK and this is their finest hour.

The first to appear at the beginning of the month is the damson blossoms, which consists of small, white flowers, similar to blackthorn but more fulsome. On the road between Leominster and Worcester there is a wonderful stretch of rolling countryside, marked by small fields and isolated farmsteads, where the hedgerows are lined with damson trees. Throughout winter they are small, scrawny

SOWING SEED OUTSIDE

Although patience at this time of year is certainly a virtue, if the ground has been dug and manured over winter then, inevitably, some of it will be ready for sowing by mid-April and the weather will be right to do it. As good a guide as any are the arrival of weed seedlings. If they can germinate and grow, then so can most hardy vegetables.

Everything depends on the state of your soil rather than the weather, because if the soil is in good condition then there is bound to be good sowing weather in April. Unless you are lucky enough to inherit perfect soil from previous owners, the process of conditioning it is one of constant improvement. What really matters is the regular addition of well-rotted organic material. We use spent mushroom compost in the vegetable garden rather than manure because it is easier and more pleasant to handle, a delivery is never more than a phone call away and it is very quickly incorporated into the soil, which means that you can mix it into the top 6 inch of ground and sow seeds the same day. On our rather heavy soil it lightens the texture better than manure, which in a wet year can make the ground even more sticky initially, although it only does good in the long run. The one disadvantage of mushroom compost is that it is rather alkaline, so if you are on chalk or limestone this may take your soil pH too high above the ideal 6.5 for most vegetables. Manure, however, tends to be slightly acidic, so the addition of farmyard manure dug in deeply every three years gets the balance about right.

But anything – manure, garden compost, composted straw as well as green manures – dug into the ground is going to improve the texture and nutritional content of the soil. The texture will steadily improve over the years but the nutrition is exhausted rapidly by heavy cropping and has to be renewed at least annually. Tests indicate that a 6 inch layer of good manure is needed every year to maintain a good standard of nutrition. This is a lot and not very practical, so we always rake in a good handful of organic fertilizer as we prepare the ground in spring, as well as a handful of

Opposite top My test for judging if the ground is sufficiently prepared for seed sowing is to see if I can easily draw a line (or drill) in the soil with my finger. *Opposite bottom* Tip a small amount of seed into the palm of one hand and take pinches with the fingers of the other. *Above* Well-spaced seedlings emerging from the soil.

dried blood for the crops that need a lot of nitrogen, like spinach and lettuce. Calcified seaweed is also good, not just as a source of slow-release nitrogen and potash, but also because it seems to help break down our heavy soil.

If you leave the ground in clods after winter digging, the combination of rain and frost breaks it down to a remarkable degree and all it will need is forking over or rototilling to level it and get a smooth surface before raking it to a fine tilth. If I cannot draw easily on the surface of the soil with my finger, it either needs further raking or forking, or else the ground is too wet.

The finger forking has relevance because I always draw the drills for the seed with a finger, not bothering with a line or rod to get them straight. I do it by eye, as I also judge the gaps between rows. Our beds are all small enough for this to be the easiest and quickest way. But by the middle of April I do have a very dirty, scarred forefinger.

The following system works for me as the easiest and quickest way to sow thinly and evenly. Pour enough seeds into one hand so that you can comfortably cup and clench your fist around them. Straddle the row or kneel next to it, take a pinch of seed between thumb and forefinger and gradually dribble it into the drill by rubbing thumb and forefinger together, moving slowly down the line. If the seed is small, like all lettuce, carrot or chicory seed, you will find that the seed in your cupped hand works into the lines on your palm, but tipping it from one hand to the other a couple of times somehow always sorts this out, leaving a neat pile to pinch.

When the seed is sown I go back down each drill, quickly closing the soil over it using thumb and forefinger again. Very often, you find that you do not want to use all the seed in the packet – turning the top over and closing it with a paper clip keeps it sealed satisfactorily.

It is absolutely vital to label each row clearly with the full name of the seed and the date sown. This is particularly useful if the seed is slow to germinate or has problems later on. If the soil is a little wet or heavy, it can be useful to draw the drill a little deeper and put a layer of vermiculite in the bottom, then cover the seeds with vermiculite when you have sown them.

Row covers and a layer of mulch will ward off most night frosts and the more damaging cold winds. What cannot be avoided is the cold rain that often comes, but it is worth taking a risk. Certainly, parsnips, carrots, lettuce of all kinds at 10-day intervals throughout the month, peas, broad beans, onion and shallot sets, radishes, beets, parsley, chard, spinach and rocket should all be sown if possible. Potatoes can go in any time from early March onward, but April is the most likely time to get them planted. Sow rocket and radishes between the rows, for a quick harvest before the potatoes need earthing up in mid-May.

THYME

Thyme is easy to grow from seed, but the plants take a year to develop sufficiently to cut regularly from, so it is a good idea to buy some plants until your own mature. A packet of seed a year will provide more than enough fresh plants to keep a household in as much thyme as they might conceivably want.

Sow the seed in a seed tray in the greenhouse, transplanting them into another seed tray when they are large enough to handle so that each tiny plant has some space to grow. These can then be put in a cold frame or a sheltered spot outside and left for a month or more. Ideally, they should be potted on into individual pots before the roots start to mat together in the seed tray, but the plants are very tough and they can be torn apart or cut with a knife without any damage being done. We once left a couple of trays of thyme seedlings for a full year, all but abandoned, but they were planted out and became fine, bushy plants eventually.

Thyme needs lots of sunshine and grows best if the soil is well drained, even thin, so do not enrich the soil, save to encourage drainage. It is especially important that thyme does not sit in wet soil in winter. Trim plants after flowering to keep them compact and producing plenty of leaves.

INDIVIDUAL HERB OMELETTE

When the hens start to lay again in spring, I like to make a fresh omelette with the young shoots of herbs. It is a beautiful combination of ocher yellow and bright green. We often eat this in the evening after working all day in the garden, when we are too tired to cook a proper meal. It depends upon the absolute freshness of the ingredients to make it special. I find two eggs rich enough, but Montagu makes his omelette using three.

2–3 eggs
Oil or butter for frying
2 tablespoons chopped fresh herbs (parsley, chives,
    golden marjoram)
Sea salt and pepper
Serves 1

Lightly beat the eggs with a fork in a mixing bowl. Heat the oil or butter in an omelette pan. It should be quite hot, hot enough for the butter to froth but not to burn. Pour in the eggs and then, as the omelette begins to cook on the base, use the fork to draw it aside and allow the uncooked egg to run beneath. Do this until the omelette sets but is still soft. Scatter the herbs on the top, season and serve. An omelette takes just a couple of minutes to cook.

BAKED CUSTARD

1 oz unsalted butter
6–10 small fresh bay leaves
3 large eggs
3 egg yolks
3 oz caster or granulated sugar
2½ cups milk
Serves 6–10 (depending upon the size of the
    individual dishes)
Oven temperature: 350°F

Butter the individual custard dishes. Place a bay leaf on the bottom of each one.

Beat the eggs, yolks and the sugar together in a bowl. Warm the milk to just below boiling point and pour onto the egg mixture, whisking continuously as you do so. Strain through a sieve, and pour into the individual dishes.

Place them in a baking pan and pour hot water in to come about halfway up the side of the dishes. Bake in the preheated oven for 1 hour or until the custards are almost set. The custards will be still quite wobbly when you take them out.

Allow them to cool for an hour after you take them out of the oven, then refrigerate for several hours before serving.

MAY

MAY IS THE BEST OF TIMES. It is like being in love. All senses are quickened to a point of almost unbearable sensitivity. The green of the new leaves shines with a cathedral intensity. Every moment in the garden is precious, and to miss a day – as so many days are missed to work or duty – is an irretrievable deprivation.

This state of clear-headed intoxication is signaled by the astonishing display of hawthorn ('may') blossoms and cow parsley that flows along lane and hedges for thousands of miles throughout the British Isles. To my mind, it is the most astonishing display of wildflowers to be seen in the world. The garden has nothing that can match it in scale or sheer bravura. There is a saying, "Ne'er cast a clout till the may is out," which can be translated as: "Don't take your winter woollies off until the hawthorn blossom is out." This used to happen around the first of the month – May Day – and was an important fertility celebration. Since the introduction of the Gregorian calendar, in 1762, when 11 days were "taken away," the blossom appears on or around the 11th of May, a date when gardeners in this part of the world can reasonably expect there to be no more frosts.

The good weather is filled with a rich, bosomy sunlight, and the odd rainy, cold day is tolerated as a mere hiccup. It might (and surprisingly often does) snow in May, but nothing stays for more than a day or so. The weather in May is a moving train taking you to summer. You can get up at 5 AM with the light creeping in and go to bed at 10 PM, with the darkness still brighter than teatime on a December afternoon. But the really important thing, the factor that makes the heart leap, is that there is so much more to come. With hindsight, I always realize that the good days of May are as good as it gets, are heaven itself living and glowing all around you. But at the time it feels like a process toward the high days of summer. Which, I suppose, is the clichéd but apt metaphor for life: Be here now.

SATURDAY, MAY 16:
Lovely day – hot.
May blossoms outrageously beautiful.
Planted yellow zucchini at bottom of Artichoke Avenue.
Transplanted 36 'Purple Queen' French beans. Tied
up and supported fava beans.
Bought hose and fittings for greenhouse and
cold frames.
Watered everywhere.
Wild garden fantastic.
Spring garden fantastic.
Herb garden lovely.
Whole garden a joy.

For all the blitheness of spirit, wise heads watch for frost in the first week of May. Clear, warm days are followed by cold nights and I have seen this garden blighted as though sprayed with weed killer as a result of a few degrees of frost in early May killing all the new, very tender growth. This is the time of year when row covers and mulch are invaluable. Growing seedlings can be protected but it is harder to stop the fruit buds being nipped on the apple, pear and plum trees. The autumn harvest is influenced more by the events of a week or so in May than the rest of the year put together.

Experience has taught me that if you have heavy soil like ours, it is not a disaster if the vegetable garden is untouched before May. In one weekend the ground can be rototilled and seed sown that will germinate fast and grow strongly, so that by mid-July the garden will have all but caught up with the keenest March and April sower. The crops that suffer most from a late sowing are garlic, spinach, rocket and potatoes. Garlic is not worth attempting to grow

unless it is in the ground by the end of February because the bulbs will not have enough time to develop before it goes to seed, spinach and rocket bolt too fast in warmth, and potatoes are liable to blight when grown organically, so the earlier they are planted the more mature they will be before blight strikes.

The main problem for the kitchen throughout May is that, however early you sow your seeds in spring, unless you have crops growing in a greenhouse or cold frame, there is a distinct shortage of things to eat. It is a lean month. Therefore, whatever you *can* harvest is doubly valued. We always eat all the thinnings of the earliest lettuces, even the very tiniest ones. The corn salad and rocket should still be providing a few small salads, but the truth is that every leaf is treasured.

Early May is a good time to sow peas of all kinds for picking in midsummer, but if it is not too cold I always try to make at least one earlier sowing as soon as I can get the soil suitably prepared in March or April. These earlier crops will be coming through and should be staked as soon as all seedlings have emerged from the ground, although germination can take as long as two weeks from the first to the last in a row of peas. The absolute rule when supporting any kind of plant is to do it before it is necessary. Initially, the support looks rather overpowering, but too little is far worse than too much.

The best thing to use to hold up peas is the traditional one of peasticks – the twiggy tops and side branches of coppiced hazel cut for beansticks and hurdles – stuck in on either side of the row so that the flat plane of the twigs fans parallel to the peas. These can be tricky to get hold of, so netting fixed securely to posts will do, although it does not look so good. Peas have twining tendrils that will attach themselves to whatever they find, and if they find nothing will create a thoroughly entwined mound. This makes picking tricky, so you want them to grow as vertically as possible, which will also ensure that all the peas get a chance to ripen.

Fava beans have no tendrils with which to cling to a support, so the best way to stop them from flopping in heavy rain or high wind is to stake around each double row with 6 foot canes and to tie string from cane to cane, starting about 24 inches off the ground and adding further rows of string at 12 inch intervals as the beans grow.

The outdoor tomatoes are not planted out until June, but in the middle of May the tomatoes and basil that were sown in March are planted out into the unheated greenhouse. Most go into beds, but we also grow some tomatoes, peppers, melons and eggplants in pots and grow bags in a separate section that can be kept slightly warmer and damper than the tomatoes really like. This always feels like a mini corner turned, signaling that you trust the weather not to get too cold again before at least September. 'Shirley' tomatoes do very well on our organic, largely laissez-faire regime, and 'Alicante' and 'Gardener's Delight' will provide a good supply of medium and small fruits. 'Buffalo' are enormous and fun, and 'Costoluto Fiorentino' is an exceptionally good beefsteak tomato. All of these will grow outside but are better in a well-ventilated cool greenhouse. The basil, such a natural and important companion to tomato on the plate, is planted in rows flanking the path between the borders, partly because it thrives in the same conditions as the tomatoes and partly because it helps deter whitefly.

The soil in the borders inside the greenhouse is very shallow and lies over an old cobbled hay yard. The tomatoes do not seem to mind this, but we do remove the top 3 inches every year and replace it with a mixture of loam, mushroom compost and composted bark. This gets rid of any lingering fungal "nasties" and rejuvenates the nutritional value of the soil. It is dressed with a good sprinkling of bonemeal and calcified seaweed a week or so before planting.

The outdoor seedbed should get filled up in May. All the brassicas, be they summer, autumn or winter, can have an initial sowing. As with lettuce, it is better to have a series of sowings so that the winter crops will provide their harvest in succession, rather than in one unusable glut.

MAKING A SEEDBED

A seed bed is the easiest and best way to raise hardy plants before transplanting them to their final position in the garden. It need not take up much room – 3 x 5 feet would be a useful size. The idea is to sow the seed in short rows that can be much closer together than if the seeds are sown *in situ*, so a rectangular shape with the rows running across the short side is best. Give your seedbed an open but protected site. Too often it is tucked away in a corner, but it is an important part of the garden. Seeds in bright light grow stronger and make better plants than those that are shaded.

The soil should be dug deeply and then left to settle. Fork it over lightly when the ground is dry enough to walk on in spring and weed it very carefully. I add plenty of sharp sand to our seedbed to ensure good drainage on our heavy soil – gravel would be too coarse for the tiny roots of seedlings. Rake it to a fine tilth. This is something that experience teaches you to recognize: The soil should not be dust and yet should have no clumps of soil bigger than a pea. If you have very heavy or wet soil, consider using a layer of vermiculite or sharp sand in the bottom of each drill.

Sow your seeds as thinly as you can, whether they are tiny like lettuce or chunky like beans. Even the smallest seedling will be better for a gap of at least 1 inch from its neighbor and it takes less time to sow thinly than to thin evenly later on.

You do not need many plants in production at any one time – after all, a daily "crop" of fresh vegetables for even a large family or party is only going to require a handful of plants. Try to sow small amounts at a time, give them the best conditions so that they grow fast, plant them out as soon as you can and sow more seed immediately once the ground is free. This way, you will achieve a rolling supply of ingredients rather than a few inconvenient gluts.

Water seedbeds very lightly. If a finely worked tilth is watered heavily and this is followed by hot, windy weather, it can form a "cap", or crust, that physically stops the emerging seedlings. This cap can also make water bounce off it and stop it from being absorbed by the soil. I know this from bitter experience. If sowing in a dry spell, water the row before you sow. The water will then be where the new roots need it – below them.

ASPARAGUS

By far the most exciting harvest of May is asparagus. Asparagus is one of those foods that are corrupted by being eaten out of season. The whole point of asparagus is that it has a time and a season. Familiarity breeds lack of proper respect for its specialness. It is one of the genuine luxury foods, in the same league as caviar, foie gras, truffles or champagne. Eating it is good not only for the taste buds but also for the spirit: It makes you feel pampered and indulged.

But if it was just indulgence you were after, then you need not go to the trouble of growing asparagus at home. That luxury can come just as well via a restaurant or the produce section in a supermarket as from your garden. But what you cannot get from almost all bought asparagus is the incredible, unique, rich taste of truly fresh spears cut within the hour of eating. For that you must either grow them yourself or buy them from a roadside seller in the Vale of Evesham and cook them by the road on a camping stove. I have done this and it is a superb way to eat it, but not always convenient.

It seems to me that asparagus, far from being a rich man's luxury, redolent of days when vast armies of gardeners served delicacies to the "big house," is one of the most practical and suitable foods to grow in the modern garden. Although it takes some time, work and knowledge to make the asparagus bed and to nurture the young plants, once they are established they will provide a spring treat for a number of years to come, with practically no attention. I would class the investment of an asparagus bed in the same way as I would the planting of a superb pear like 'Doyenné du Comice'.

Having said this, I failed miserably in my first attempt to grow asparagus. Like most people, I had not grown it because I thought that it would be too long before we got any return, and I was always in a hurry. But we stopped at the roadside stall just outside Evesham on our way back from visiting Rousham, William Kent's masterpiece just north of Oxford. The stall was set up at the edge of a whole field of asparagus to sell the first freshly cut asparagus of the year. It was a cold, gray mid-April day, but the combination of Rousham and asparagus was exhilarating.

Until 20 years ago the best asparagus came from this small region. It was cut at dawn and sent by train to market the same day so that it could be in your local produce market the next morning. Now the supermarkets import it by the ton from Europe, and Evesham asparagus growers are a dying breed.

Asparagus has a fearsome reputation as being tortuously slow to produce a harvestable crop and requiring specialist treatment lavished on it. When I began growing vegetables myself I was put off growing the stuff by the photographs in the 1961 edition of the Royal Horticultural Society's *The Vegetable Garden Displayed* – which for years was my vegetable bible. This shows the required planting trench as having the profile of a W, so that the bottom of the trench had a ridge running along its length. This was done with such terrifying crispness that I didn't even dare try digging it – let alone planting the asparagus roots along its ridge and waiting three years before cutting shoots (for precisely six weeks the first year and eight weeks the second). Brilliant expertise or unnecessary bullshit? Not only was it difficult, it was also dauntingly long term. The great attraction of vegetable growing is that you can take an uncultivated patch of planet and dig it, sow seeds, tend them, harvest and eat them within one growing season. If it does not work you can try the whole procedure again next year and with a number of vegetables, within a matter of months. This year's failures are next year's experience. But asparagus might sit there like a threat for years, without ever either providing a good crop or giving you the chance to experiment.

However, when we stopped to get some asparagus for supper, I also bought four dozen 'F1' plants, persuaded by the grower that they could just be planted "normally" in any good soil and that I would be harvesting a few good spears from each plant in a year's time. He did add, slightly ominously, that I must keep them well watered "if they are to take." "Taking" always implies a breathless period when the plant balances on a tightrope of living and dying. It is a time for crossed fingers and Emergency Care. Whenever I get a plant I have never grown before, I look it up in the various reference books I have. The advice all agreed on the

need for really good drainage, although the degree ranged from the cautionary to the severe, with one instructing me to: "incorporate much old rubble, grit and bonfire soil. On top of this, and above the level of the surrounding soil, place a layer of very sandy, gritty soil; a load of sandy aggregate from a seaside quarry is ideal.... This aggregate mixed with leaf mold, peat or fine compost and bonfire soil is the planting mixture...." Phew!

Nevertheless, I dug my new asparagus patch deeply and shoveled 12 inches of topsoil from two bordering paths to double the height of the soil. I planted the asparagus in a block at 12 inch spacing, watered them well, kept them watered and spent a month watching them not taking.

The following season, we cut about a dozen spears from our four dozen plants; not a success. But the reason was obvious. That corner of the vegetable garden is the sunniest but also the first to flood, and recent conditions had been so wet that it had flooded half a dozen times since planting. However good the drainage, asparagus will not like that. So in June I dug up the plants, potted them up and will make a new asparagus patch in a raised bed at a drier spot. And this time I will make it *very* well drained.

If you do manage to get the crowns to "take," you should leave them to develop their distinctive, feathery foliage. This stays until November, when it turns yellow, and this is the time to cut it back to the ground. It is important to do this before any ripe berries drop to the ground, as Sod's law says that these will be female, germinate and take like a rocket, crowding the bed and thus diminishing the crop. Only the male plants produce spears. But you can buy all-male hybrid seeds or plants.

You can now also get asparagus seed that will produce a crop of spears just one year after sowing. In the UK, Thompson & Morgan sell a cultivar named 'Jersey Knight Improved' and they claim, in the quaintly Victorian poster style common to most seed catalog: "Within eight weeks of starting seed indoors, you'll have a healthy young transplant... and by the following spring it will be large enough to produce a harvest of juicy, vitamin-rich spears – *a year ahead of year-old roots.* Under normal conditions."

I have a sneaking suspicion that the last qualifying sentence might mean truckloads of sandy aggregate from a seaside quarry, bonfire soil, leaf mold and much old rubble, but I am all for anything that will simplify the growing process so that more people get a chance to eat homegrown vegetables. You get 10 seeds in a packet and you can reckon that, when mature, these will produce enough spears for a dish for two people every week throughout May.

The British grow the green variety of *Asparagus officinalis*, whose green shoots are topped by purple heads and are succulent right down the stem, but asparagus growers on the Continent mainly grow the white type, thicker and coarser, which is further blanched by being grown in a deep trench and harvested when only the tips appear above ground. There is also a purple type. There is no great difference between them and the varieties that you are likely to find as plants do not show any great range of characteristics. 'Accell' produces all-male seeds, 'Giant Mammoth' is better adapted for heavy soil, and 'Connover's Colossal' is early and heavy cropping when grown on sandy soil. 'Martha Washington' is an American variety that has long spears and is rust-resistant, and 'Lucullus' also has long, slim spears.

William Cobbett, that most truculent of heroes, would have none of this differentiation: "As to the sorts of asparagus of which some people talk, I, for my part, could never discover any difference...." In his time (the early nineteenth century) it was a wildly popular vegetable with 260 acres of asparagus fields in Battersea alone and the asparagus beds in the walled gardens of country houses often taking up half an acre – which would absorb three or four average-sized gardens now. To increase production the plants were rested for a month in June and then manured heavily, so that they would produce another crop of spears in September.

A last word on asparagus. Everybody who eats asparagus creates a chemical reaction that is unique to the plant. The sulfur-containing amino acid methionine in the asparagus causes a secretion of methyl mercaptan, which is what makes your urine smell so distinctly within minutes of eating.

SPINACH

The one "proper" salad that can nearly always be squeezed out of May is one of spinach and bacon. These first raw spinach leaves are as good as anything that enters your mouth. Spinach grows its leaves back if picked, although it is always a race against too much hot weather, as it is very prone to bolting as soon as the weather warms up. Unlike its cousin chard, once spinach starts to bolt it is unsalvageable. Best to pull up what is left, use what you can and put the remainder on the compost heap to use the ground for lettuces, which are not so sensitive to heat.

Spinach needs to grow fast and therefore wants rich soil with plenty of nitrogen. This can come from manure if you have it, but a dressing of dried blood or pelleted, concentrated manure just before sowing will undoubtedly help. It also needs lots of water.

The time to sow it is in March and/or April, preferably warming the soil with a mulch or row covers for a week first so that it will germinate. Sow thinly in rows 12 inches apart and thin the seedlings to 3 inch spacings. Spinach is especially popular with slugs and snails, which can strip a row of seedlings overnight, so you have to keep an eye on this (although, short of using noxious slug pellets, there is little you can do to stop the horrible things taking their pick if they have a mind to).

'Sigmaleaf' is a reliable variety that produces deliciously juicy leaves. While, in theory, you could sow spinach under cover and then transplant it, I see little point as this would check growth and the point is to get pickable leaves as soon as possible. By June the leaves have gotten coarser and are best cooked.

ORACHE

Orache is a kind of spinach with rather different habits. It can be sown in the same manner and at the same time as "normal" spinach, but will develop more slowly. There are both green and red varieties, both of which produce heart-shaped leaves that look and taste good, although I think that the red looks better and tastes every bit as good as the green. You should eat the leaves when they are very young and tender, because the plant will then develop into a purple-stemmed monster that will stay in alizarin leaf until late October and whose seeds stay in the ground for years. But it is hardly a weed, as it is good looking, edible and terribly easy to pull up. We deliberately scatter it in certain parts of the flower garden, along with poppy seeds, as welcome invaders.

SPRING GREENS

Spring greens can be – should be – delicious. One of the most memorably tasty meals of my life was eaten at a friend's house on the first of May and consisted of a roast rib of Aberdeen Angus beef, spring greens and plain boiled, floury potatoes. This was followed by a rhubarb crumble. Every ingredient was perfectly prepared and superb on its own, and all the component parts wedded perfectly together. This is the message that is at the heart of this book: Food is at its best when the ingredients are absolutely fresh and prepared as simply and carefully as possible.

Actually, there is no vegetable called "spring greens". There are two types of cabbage that develop in spring: The one we call spring greens has loose leaves, while spring cabbage has a more solid heart. To make matters even more confusing, we grow a variety called 'Durham Early', which is edible both loose leaved and again when it hearts up. 'Spring Hero' also has this dual capacity.

But the good, loose-leaved spring greens are a treat. You can have solid cabbage all winter and most of the summer. Spring greens belong to April and May and should be relished as a seasonal treat. I have not yet grown, but intend

to try, the Northern Irish spring cabbage 'Delaway', which has cut-and-come-again leaves and is the original basis for colcannon and cabbage and bacon – both very Irish dishes.

Spring greens are smooth and loose on the plate – eating them is somewhere between eating cabbage and lettuce. They should, above all, taste fresh and bright and not at all like the residue of a winter of boiled cabbages.

However, for all their potential zinginess in the mouth, they need to grow slowly throughout winter. We sow the seed in a seedbed in early August, thinning them to about

4 inches apart as soon as this is practical. They then develop into strong but small plants that go into their place in the garden in early October. They are planted rather closer together than winter cabbages – 12 inches in each direction should give them enough room – as you are after the loose, fresh growth rather than big, solid hearts.

Over the year that this book was photographed, the 'Durham Early' were planted into the aborted asparagus bed, following outdoor 'Gardener's Delight' tomatoes and basil that had spent the summer there. Unlike the winter cabbages, which mature steadily from planting out, these grow very slowly over the winter before making a burst of growth in spring – which accounts for the freshness of taste.

Summer cabbages should be sown outside in early May (or a month or two earlier under cover) for harvesting in July and August. You have to like cabbage a lot to grow it as a summer vegetable; it will compete with the other more conventionally summery crops, but a few do not go amiss. They look good, too, with globes of pale green against the brown soil.

NETTLE SOUP

SUNDAY, MAY 31:

Was outside working by 6 AM weeding onion sets and
  asparagus....

... mulched around strawberries last thing with gravel –
  five bags – mainly to deter slugs as well as to keep
  fruits clean. Became too dark to see by 10:30 PM....

NETTLE SOUP

In spring the young shoots of nettles are tender and
nutritious and you can quickly pick enough for soup – but
you must wear rubber gloves. You pick the top of the
young shoots only – the first two leaves and the bud. They
cook down rather like spinach and lose all their sting. You
can substitute spinach for nettles.

8 oz young nettle shoots (or young spinach leaves)

4 oz butter

1 lb onions, sliced

6 cloves garlic, chopped

5 cups vegetable or chicken stock

Sea salt and pepper

4 oz crème fraîche

Serves 6

Wash the nettle shoots. Melt the butter in a large saucepan
and fry the onions gently over a low heat for about 10
minutes until translucent. Add the garlic, and cook gently
with the onions for 2 minutes. Add the nettles and the stock
and bring up to a boil. Gently simmer for 5 minutes, then
purée the soup to a smooth green purée. Season generously
with salt and pepper. Serve hot with a dollop of crème
fraîche in each bowl.

SPINACH, ORACHE AND BACON SALAD

Before all the lettuce starts to come in June, this is a really good late-spring salad.

1 bunch of baby spinach
1 bunch of young tender red orache leaves
4 oz smoked streaky bacon
2–3 tablespoons olive oil
2 slices white bread
1 tablespoon balsamic vinegar
Serves 6

Wash and dry the spinach and orache leaves, and put them into a big salad bowl.

Cut the bacon into fine strips, and fry in a little olive oil until crispy. Remove from the pan. Add some more olive oil to the bacon juices in the pan. Remove the crusts from the bread and cut into 10mm ($\frac{1}{2}$in) cubes. Fry until lightly browned all over.

Assemble the salad at the last moment by dressing it with the balsamic vinegar, and scattering the bacon and croûtons on top.

CRUMBLE

This is a homey and easy pudding. It looks so appetizing with the juices bubbling up through the golden crust. Best served with homemade custard or ice cream.

2$\frac{1}{4}$ lbs fruit (apples, plums, damsons,
raspberries, gooseberries, rhubarb)
Sugar
For the crumble topping
8 oz unbleached plain flour
4 oz unsalted butter
4 oz sugar
Serves 6 with leftovers
Oven temperature: 375°F

Process the flour and butter, then mix in the sugar. The mixture should look like bread crumbs.

Prepare the fruit – peel and slice apples; leave plums, damsons and raspberries whole; top and tail gooseberries; cut rhubarb into 2 inch chunks. Put the fruit in an ovenproof dish. Sprinkle with sugar to taste and a little water if necessary for firm fruits such as apples. Pour the crumble mixture over the top of the fruit. Loosely level it, but don't pack it down. Bake in the preheated oven for about 30 minutes.

Variation Replace up to half the flour with ground hazelnuts or ground almonds.

POURING CUSTARD

I like to have little flecks of vanilla in my custard. It is absolutely delicious poured over stewed apples or plums, pies and crumbles. I find this is sweet enough, but add more sugar if you prefer.

4 large egg yolks
2 oz caster or granulated sugar
$\frac{1}{2}$ vanilla pod, split open
18 fl oz full whole milk
4$\frac{1}{2}$ fl oz heavy cream
Serves 6

Whisk the eggs yolks and sugar together in a bowl.

Scrape the inner black sticky seeds from the vanilla pod half, and add to the milk in a saucepan. Heat the milk to just below boiling, then leave to stand off the heat for about 5 minutes to develop the flavor of the vanilla.

Pour the milk over the eggs and sugar, whisking continuously. Return to the heat in a double boiler, and stir with a wooden spoon until the sauce thickens. Be careful not to overheat, or the mixture will separate into grainy lumps. Stir in the cream.

Pour into a jug to serve warm.

JUNE

ALTHOUGH THE CALENDAR might tell you that June is midsummer, for the gardener there is a period lying between spring and summer from roughly two-thirds of the way through May until midsummer, which is "early summer." It is a separate season. There is none of the lushness that characterizes mid- and late summer and, by the same token, none of the heavy, slightly worn sense of exposure. Everything still shines. Florally, it is the month of the Old Roses, outside the scope of this book but very much inside the heart of this garden. But despite their astonishing, subtle brilliance, June is a green time, and here in the west of England the grass, hedgerows, trees, borders and vegetable garden are dominated by scores of different greens. You can read a book outside at 10 PM, sleep a little and continue reading again by natural light at 4:30 AM. This gives June the luxury of time on a scale that no other month has. Even if you have to work all day, there is still the chance of three hours outside before bed. This makes up for the dismal hibernation in of midwinter afternoons.

But the vegetable garden, at the beginning of the month at any rate, is surprisingly incomplete. Most things are still growing, with the weeds growing faster than anything else. It is a month busy with weeding, thinning and planting out rather than harvesting. But what there is to harvest is special and satisfying enough. Asparagus can still be cut until the middle of the month, when the remaining spears should be left to grow and nurture the roots. Artichokes, good from May to October, are at their new best in June. Broad beans, too, are at their prime, as are gooseberries and, of course, lettuce. June is the lettuce month, warm enough to make them grow fast and yet rarely so hot as to hurry them into untimely bolting. I like to boast that we can pick a salad from the garden every day of the year, yet that rather depends on how many people are going to be fed. In June we are spoiled for choice. It is easy – it wants to grow. A crisp cos (or romaine) lettuce, with leaves curved inward like the hull of a boat, some chives and marjoram, good oil and balsamic vinegar and you have the basis for a meal eaten as the light fades around 10 PM. It takes less than five minutes from conception to execution.

June is when all the tender vegetables like tomatoes, basil, squashes, French beans, runner beans, sweet corn, celery, cucumbers and cardoons can safely be planted out. This clears the greenhouse and cold frames, which, by the beginning of the month, are becoming completely cluttered. Because all these plants take a week or so to adjust and start to grow it is essential to keep them weeded and watered, so the careful tending goes from inside to out. The onions, too, whether in the form of seed, onion sets, shallots or garlic, all have to be kept weed-free, as they are very sensitive to competition of any kind and weeds will dramatically reduce the amount that they swell at this stage.

It is a too-often repeated truism that a weed is only a plant where you do not want it; crowding the plants that you *do* want has exactly the same effect as letting the weeds dominate a row or block of a precious harvest. So you must thin, allowing each plant enough space, water and nutrients to develop fully and healthily. It is best to do this little and often and, wherever possible, eat the thinnings. For some vegetables this is not possible, but for others, like baby carrots, lettuces and onions, it is a treat.

Throughout the month we sow small quantities of every kind of lettuce, including curly endive and radicchio – which are both types of chicory but which we grow as bitter salad leaves. The real chicories, which are essentially winter crops, can also be sown in June so they can grow slowly throughout the summer and be ready for harvesting from October onward. I sow more parsley to cover us for the

winter, and more cabbages so that they will be ready for planting out in August.

The new potatoes will be growing vigorously and starting to flower from the end of the month, depending on when they were planted. I earth them up at the end of May or beginning of June, drawing the soil from in between the rows round the top growth, both to protect it and to cover any potatoes forming near the surface, which would otherwise spoil from exposure to light.

The celery and celeriac can be planted out midmonth and watered thereafter almost daily. It is tempting to plant these out earlier in May or early June but all experience shows that it is better to plant them around the longest day and then let them grow fast.

The first leeks go out, poor wispy things that they are, leaning against the edges of their dibbed planting holes, but perfectly happy to be there.

In the unheated greenhouse the tomatoes have to be weeded, watered, fed, tied to their supporting canes as they grow and the side shoots nipped out. I try to spend half an hour there each Saturday morning, going over each plant. The outdoor tomatoes are grown as bushes rather than trained but need to be staked and tied all the same, to protect them from wind damage as much as anything else.

In the herb garden the lovage, fennel and angelica dominate, towering above the rest. The parsley that saw us through the winter and spring has to be dug up and chucked, and the spring-sown batch just starts to give a few leaves. The sage is flowering and putting on vigorous growth following its hard pruning in April. The mint growing in the two old cattle troughs outside the back door is growing strongly, too. Of all the places of the garden, this, the herb garden, demands least attention other than use and admiration.

Which is a relief, because it is a busy, busy time.

TUESDAY, JUNE 9:
Bone tired. Good for nothing.

ZUCCHINIS

A zucchini or courgette (same thing) is merely a baby marrow. All these things are summer squashes. What distinguishes them from winter squashes is their thin skin and a slightly hardier constitution that enables them to be planted out and to start producing edible fruit earlier in the year. But they share the squash's need for lots of rich soil and water.

In June you get the wonderful little zucchini the size of sausages, and if you keep cutting them they will produce more almost indefinitely until the first frosts. If you leave them they will expand out to the size of long balloons and not be worth their space in the kitchen.

I sow them in early April, two seeds to a 6 inch pot, in the greenhouse, removing the weaker of the two plants if they both germinate. There is no need to transplant them or pot them, and they should be ready for planting out 3 feet apart in the middle of May, but they must be hardened off via a cold frame and then in a sheltered spot outside for a week before planting out. If there is a frost after this date they will die, but that is a risk worth taking, especially if you keep a couple of plants back until the weather is cast iron. Within a month they will be producing their harvest. Easy.

WEDNESDAY, JUNE 10:
Very strong southwesterly wind. Destructive.
Dug up asparagus (seven plants) and potted up. Dug
   new plot. Very sticky. Added four bags of gravel.
... put the green basil out to harden off.
Chard and pasta for dinner.

LETTUCE

Of all the things to grow in the garden, lettuce is probably the easiest and most useful. It can be grown in grow bags, window boxes, a spare piece of flower border or even a hanging basket. Although it is ubiquitous, good lettuce is all too rarely experienced outside a garden. Yes, lettuce usually accompanies "fast food," and millions of iceberg lettuces are eaten throughout the Western world each week, but most of the eaters are unaware of it and those who notice it pay little attention or interest to the variety or taste. If it is an iceberg lettuce, then it will have no taste at all beyond a familiar damp crispness.

However, there are hundreds of different varieties of lettuce. Most seed catalogs have between one and two dozen different varieties, and even the most limited garden center should have a reasonable selection. My favorite is cos (also called romaine), and the best cos are 'Lobjoits Green' and 'Little Gem', both of which are easy to grow. 'Little Gem' is smaller and sweeter, but 'Lobjoits' is marvelous and, if eaten young and grown fast, is unsurpassable. 'Valmaine' is an American cos or romaine and much used for Caesar salad (although I have eaten abominations in the name of that dish, using tasteless icebergs). 'Winter Density', 'Barcarolle' and 'Rouge d'Hiver' are also all cos.

Butterhead, or round, lettuces have flat, rounded heads and soft leaves. They are not fashionable but the whole point of growing food at home is to have a range and variety that you can dip into like a pick 'n' mix counter. 'Tom Thumb' is a very good butterhead, small (about the size of a tennis ball), sweet and full of taste. The seeds are an idiosyncratic black.

The crisphead, or iceberg, lettuces, easy villains of mass production, are worth growing to see what they can really taste like and to know that they are chemically "clean." 'Mini Green' is another tennis-ball-sized lettuce, rather crisper than 'Tom Thumb'. 'Webb's Wonderful', probably the best-known crisphead, was bred directly from it, but is not so wonderful. 'Chou de Naples' is the parent of most modern iceberg lettuces and has the great virtue of being slow to bolt.

The final type of lettuce is the loose-leaved type. These have no heart but consist of a mass of 'loose' leaves that can be picked individually either piecemeal or by cutting the whole lot. Either way, they will regrow and three pickings should be possible if the lettuce gets enough water. The most famous – and nastiest – is 'Lollo Rossa'. Much better are the 'Salad Bowl' and 'Oak Leaf' types. If regularly picked over these can last for months, the stems gradually growing longer and the leaves becoming less prominent but remaining edible almost until Christmas. I never know if it is better to pick a little from a lot of plants or to strip a plant completely in order to maximize production. It is an academic question really, because for much of the year we have too much lettuce. The only drawback to 'Salad Bowl' lettuces are that they can be rather slimy when dressed; better to eat them with a dribble of oil and lemon juice put directly onto the plate than mixed in the salad bowl.

Red lettuce became trendy with the vogue of the kitchen garden and they are very pretty as well as delicious. 'Red Salad Bowl', 'Red Oak Leaf', 'Merveille de Quatre Saisons' and 'Red Cos' are all good.

Bolting, or running to seed, is a problem with nearly all lettuces when exposed to heat or drought. Invariably, from mid-June to mid-August, there will be a sowing of lettuces that are growing nicely but have not formed a decent enough body to justify picking; you keep a beady eye on them, take a few, find them delicious, go away for the weekend and come back to find that the whole lot are starting to bolt.

Bolting is a defense mechanism whereby the plant senses drought (and therefore death) and puts on a burst of growth to produce seed quickly to preserve the species before it expires. Regular watering will help, as will providing some shade, especially in the middle of the day. But the best weapon against bolting is to sow only a few seeds at a time and to do so at 10-day intervals. Most lettuces take between about a month and 6 weeks to grow sufficiently large to eat, and will last for 8 to 10 weeks after sowing if kept watered and cool. The ideal is to have them growing at every stage of their development at any given time, rather than a glut. Also, adequate thinning and weeding will mean that the lettuces are not competing for

water. Lettuces need cool temperatures to germinate, and may become dormant if the soil temperature is above 68°F. They like a rich soil with good drainage.

Most lettuces are best sown in drills about 1/2 inch deep as thinly as possible. It is not a bad idea to water the drill before you sow the seed, so that they lie on wet ground. In about a week a green rash will spread down the drill line. As soon as they are big enough, they will need thinning. The initial thinning is best done by reducing the width of the row to one plant if possible. It varies from variety to variety, but I would say that no lettuce needs to be more than 6 inches apart. It is far better to have two small plants than one whopper. Even tiny thinnings can be eaten, by the dozen, roots and all, and are very good. The secret is not to regard thinning as a one-time only job, but to do it every week, so that the plants gradually have more space and water as they grow bigger and you waste neither plants nor growing space.

If the weather is damp and overcast, I often transplant young thinnings. You need to do this carefully, to extract as much root as possible. This can be a challenge, but it automatically helps succession. However careful you are, the lettuce will be traumatized and suffer a setback of up to 14 days in growth. This is exactly what you want, creating two harvests from a group of plants the same age.

THURSDAY, JUNE 11:
Rainy start. Very cold wind all day. Wind has broken three limes.
Cold has blackened basil in the greenhouse. Still poor germination everywhere. Cold?

FAVA BEANS

I love the way that fava beans are suddenly there after weeks and months of arriving. The flowers are still appearing at the top of the plants – by now 5 feet tall – but look through the leaves and you find the fingers of beans hanging down just an inch or two long. At this stage, they

Chicory and lettuce growing in rows. Strictly speaking, these should be thinned much more drastically than this but there is a sumptuousness about this ordered fecundity that makes conventional spacing seem too puritanical. What this shows most clearly is how generous and careless you can be with the harvest from just a few cheap packets of seed.

are delicious eaten whole. Leave them for a week and the beans inside will be pea sized and at their best. Another week and they should be eaten urgently, and after a third week they are the familiar floury pebbles that were served up in my childhood as hard lumps in a gluey white sauce.

There is something about fava beans that is instantly recognizable as ancient and sustaining. They were part of the Western diet by the Iron Age and have undoubtedly been grown in this garden for as long as it has been tilled – which is at least 600 years and probably twice that long. The expression *a beano*, to indicate "a feast," comes from the 'beanfeast' that was the annual farm workers' dinner bulked out by beans. But the point about growing fava beans, in this modern world where no one needs to grow beans – or much else for that matter – to aid survival of the body so much as to satisfy the senses, is always to harvest and eat them small. This means having small quantities of beans growing in succession rather than one big crop.

They are remarkably hardy. We try to make a sowing as early as November, another in the New Year and again in March and April. Four small crops also makes rotation more flexible because, as part of the legume family, fava beans need ground that has been freshly dug and manured and are best followed by brassica crops. It is better to have small parcels of ground coming clear all the time rather than a big switch-over of crops every few months.

I always sow them in double rows. This was something that I must have been taught to do as a child and have never queried it. Looking at my reference books, I see no one else does it. Ah well; it works. I won't stop doing it now. Because the seeds are large the ground only has to be workable to the extent that you can run a rake through it. A well-worked tilth is wasted on them.

I mark the site of the rows by running a rake firmly down the line so that it forms a very shallow trench, perhaps 1 inch deep. Straddling this, walking backward, I plant the beans in pairs about 9 inches apart (the span of my outstretched hand) in both directions, pushing each bean into the ground. The soil is then raked back over them. Each double row should be about 18 inches apart – or room enough to walk between them to pick the beans.

The beans sown in autumn and midwinter will germinate and grow to a few inches tall before stopping growth until the days lengthen and the temperature rises, but will crop as much as a month earlier than the spring-sown ones. 'Aquadulce' is usually the best for an autumn or winter sowing, and 'Bunyard's Exhibition' for early spring. 'Red Epicure' has red flowers and pinky brown beans and is worth growing just for the way that it looks, although it also tastes very good.

Beans are very prone to attack by black bean aphids, which cover the tops of the plants like soot. Pinching out the top few inches as soon as beans start to appear is the best means of defense against this.

MONDAY, JUNE 15:
… I realize that a lot of seeds are damping off outside. Very odd. They germinate (badly), appear and then die.
Tomatoes hardly growing.

GOOSEBERRIES

Gooseberries manage to take us by surprise every year, being the first soft fruit to ripen. Gooseberries attract a fanatical band of growers in Britain but, predictably, for all the wrong reasons. Foolish people spend hours, and doubtless money, attempting to grow bigger and better gooseberries than anyone else, and gooseberry shows take place every June to establish the champion gooseberry and its grower.

But gooseberries are there to be savored in the mouth, be they large or small. At their best they are a wonderful mixture of acidity and sweetness, and I would readily swap a half-decent gooseberry for every watery, tasteless strawberry I have been served. Gooseberry fool is food of the gods, with gooseberry jam and gooseberry tart running pretty close behind. And gooseberry crumble. And hot gooseberry sauce with fish. And a bowl of large ripe, purple dessert gooseberries.

It is a very limiting mistake to think of gooseberries as being invariably green. They come almost white ('Langley Gage', 'Careless'), a deep wine red ('London', 'Warrington') and golden yellow ('Early Sulphur', 'Golden Drop'). Many are delicious eaten straight off the bush, with a wonderful and unique combination of firm skin and flesh and a soft, molten interior.

The best time to plant gooseberries is, as with all deciduous fruit, between November and February. Gooseberries need a high level of potash, so give them a potash feed (potassium sulfate or rock potash) in early spring and mulch well with compost or manure. We save all our ash from the log fires in the house and spread this as a mulch around each bush, putting the compost on top of it.

Growing gooseberry bushes is easy, as long as the soil is rich and there is sufficient moisture, but getting them to produce a reliable crop of berries is more tricky. There are two main problems. The first is sawfly, which can completely defoliate a gooseberry bush in days, stripping the flesh off the leaves so that only the veins are left. This will not kill the plant, but certainly eliminates any fruit for the remainder of the year and will not encourage healthy growth in the bush. The first signs of sawfly are tiny holes in the leaves, and it is essential to take immediate action when you see this. The caterpillars will be on the underside of the leaves and must all be picked off. They tend to start eating from the interior of the plant, so by the time you notice the damage it is too late.

The second problem is gray mold, which ruins the fruit and makes the bush unhealthy. Both problems are best solved by a pruning regime that opens the bush out and raises the fruiting part up off the ground. This will ventilate the bush, which is essential to avoid fungus, and also makes the fruit much easier to pick. Start by cutting out any crossing branches, and any that leave less than a 2 inch gap with their neighbors. Take out the center of the bush so that it is bowl shaped. This is never as easy as it sounds and it might take a few years to get a bush to the point at which this kind of pruning is logical rather than guesswork, but it is worth trying to get it right to get a healthy supply of lovely gooseberries.

Gooseberry bushes are best grown as standards or semi-standards, which means that the thorny branches are at least 12 inches clear of the ground. This gets air right around them, enables wind to dry the branches (the mold likes warm, damp conditions) and makes weeding very much easier. A single standard in a pot will look good and provide enough fruit for a meal.

Now, I have to confess that my gooseberries always get gray mold, although this is partly because I have not yet had the courage to prune them hard enough. My next step is to grow gooseberries as cordons, training each bush into a pair of vertical branches tied to cross wires and pruning off all side shoots so that they look like raspberry cordons. I have seen this done and although the plants are slower to establish it looks good, makes picking terribly easy and should solve the ventilation problem.

SUNDAY, JUNE 21:
Started fine and warm (windy and cloudy), stayed warm and windy.
Moved compost heap.
Planted out leeks.
Staked melons and tomatoes in top greenhouse. Fed with seaweed.
Planted out remainder of celeriac in last year's seedbed.
Did a lot of sowing in new vegetable beds. Lettuce: 'Lobjoits Green' cos, 'Green Salad Bowl', 'Tom Thumb'; beets: 'Detroit 2'; turnip: 'Snowball'; rocket, dill, four rows flat-leaf parsley, one row 'Feltham 1st' peas, ruby chard.
Planted out sweet corn, 'Autumn' squash and 'Cream of the Crop'.

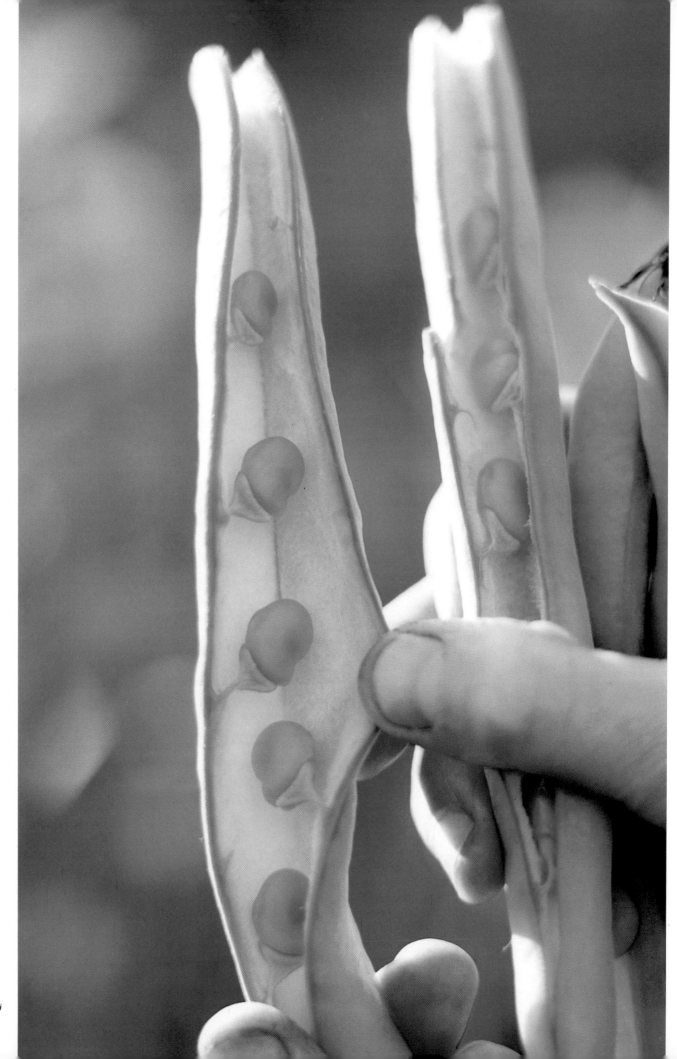

FAVA BEAN SALAD WITH BACON

Young fava beans are my favorite vegetable. When they get older they get tough and mealy and need to be popped out of their skins after cooking. Tiny fava beans in their pods, up to 4 inches long, can be blanched for 5 minutes and eaten whole.

For this recipe, use the very young tender beans, while their skins are still soft – 3 lbs 5 oz of beans in the pod, when shelled, yields about 10 1/2 oz. This is good eaten warm with a few shavings of Parmesan. I have tried local cheeses, but nothing can improve on good Parmesan.

4 oz very finely sliced dry-cured streaky bacon
Olive oil for frying
10 oz shelled fava beans
Bunch of fresh flat-leaf parsley, finely chopped
Parmesan cheese
Lemon quarters
For the dressing
1–2 tablespoons olive oil
Juice of 1/2 lemon
Sea salt and pepper
Serves 6

Cut the bacon into strips and fry in a little olive oil for about 5 minutes until it is slightly crisp. Cook the beans in boiling water for 4 minutes – less if they are very tiny. Drain the beans and dress them immediately with the olive oil and lemon juice. Season with salt and pepper. Add the bacon and parsley, and serve while still warm with shavings of Parmesan and quartered lemon. (Shave the Parmesan with a potato peeler.)

ZUCCHINIS WITH PASTA

1 lb 5oz yellow zucchinis
3 1/2 fl oz extra virgin olive oil
1 lb 5 oz fresh spaghetti
4 oz shelled fresh peas
Sea salt and black pepper
Bunch of fresh basil leaves (torn) or lemon thyme (chopped)
4 oz pecorino or similar hard cheese, cut into almost translucent slices
Serves 6

Bring a large pan of salted water to a boil.

Slice the zucchinis into 1/2 inch rounds. Cook them quickly in 1 tablespoon of the olive oil, while cooking the spaghetti in the boiling water.

Add the peas to the zucchinis to heat through.

Drain the spaghetti, pour over the vegetables and season. Serve with the cheese and herbs scattered over the surface, and the rest of the oil drizzled over.

ZUCCHINI FRITTATA

Zucchinis come in many shapes, sizes and colors, and we often eat them simply cooked in oil with garlic and fresh basil or with a tomato sauce (there are two recipes on page 56). However, I once ate them in a restaurant in a frittata, and here is my version. I have also made a similar dish using blanched chard.

1 lb 5 oz zucchinis
6 tablespoons olive oil
4 large cloves garlic, finely chopped
12 eggs
2 oz Parmesan, freshly grated
Handful of fresh basil leaves, torn
Sea salt and freshly ground black pepper
Serves 6

Coarsely grate the zucchinis into a colander, salt them lightly and leave to drain for 30 minutes. Press out the moisture.

Heat half the oil in a frying pan, and cook the garlic gently without browning it. Add the zucchinis and fry for about 5 minutes. Take from the heat and allow to cool.

Beat the eggs in a bowl, and stir in the zucchini mixture, the Parmesan, the torn basil leaves, and salt and pepper to taste.

Heat the rest of the oil in a large frying pan and, when hot, pour in the egg mixture. Lower the heat and cook slowly, stirring as the egg begins to set. When the mixture is firm, except for the top, finish it by placing it under a preheated hot grill (I use the top oven of the Aga) until it is slightly browned.

Place a plate over the top and, being careful not to burn yourself on the handle of the pan, turn the frittata out onto the plate. Serve warm, cut into wedges.

Variation Make individual frittatas in small frying pans.

GOOSEBERRY FOOL

Fruit fools can be made with custard or whipped cream. This one is made with cream because I do everything at high speed which suits my kind of cooking. I love puddings but never seem to have time to make the complicated ones. Fruit cooked in a covered dish, baked in its own juices, seems to retain the essence of the fruit. Stemming and tailing is the sort of job you can give to someone else to do while you cook, or you can take the job outside and sit in the sun.

1 lb gooseberries, stemmed and tailed

1 head of elderflowers (if available in season)

1 dessert spoon unsalted butter

4 oz golden granulated sugar, or less, to your taste

1 cup heavy cream

Serves 6

Oven temperature: 375°F

Bake the gooseberries (with the elderflower head) in a covered dish in the preheated oven for about 30 minutes until they are soft and the juices run. Remove the elderflower head (if used). Drain the fruit, reserving the juice. Purée the gooseberry pulp until smooth. I don't sieve it because I don't mind the seeds, but sieve it if you prefer. Mix in the butter together with the reserved juice and sweeten to taste while the gooseberries are still hot. Allow to cool. Whip the heavy cream and stir in the cooled gooseberry mixture.

ELDERFLOWER VINEGAR

Elderflowers steeped in white wine vinegar for a week make an aromatic vinegar for deglazing chicken juices after roasting or for summer salad dressings. Make it in any quantities you want – it keeps for ages – using these proportions. See the recipe for elderflower cordial below for picking and preparing elderflowers.

15 elderflower heads
7 cups white wine or cider vinegar
Makes 7 cups

You need a deep bowl. Put in the elderflowers, pour over the vinegar and push down the flower heads gently. Cover with a cloth and leave in a cool place for a week, stirring from time to time.

Strain through muslin, and bottle.

ELDERFLOWER CORDIAL

Pick elderflowers from trees well away from roads and traffic fumes. Smell the flowers before you pick them. Occasionally trees have an unpleasant smell like tomcats. Choose only sweetly scented flowers. This is a favorite summer drink, diluted with fizzy water. It's so popular it doesn't last long.

20 heads of elderflower
4 lbs granulated sugar
4 cups water
6 lemons
2 oz citric acid
Makes about six 17 fl oz bottles

Collect the elderflower heads and shake off any insect life, but don't wash them. Put them in a large bowl.

Put the sugar in a pan with the water and slowly bring to a boil until the sugar dissolves. Remove from the heat and allow to cool before adding the peeled zest of 4 of the lemons (peel it off using a potato peeler). Slice all 6 lemons and add to the bowl. Pour over the sugar syrup and add the citric acid. Leave for 24 hours.

Strain the cordial through double muslin and pour into sterilized bottles (I have used beer bottles with the old-fashioned metal levered caps). Store in a cool dark place (use within 3 months).

JULY

THE WHOLE GARDENING YEAR hinges upon the end of the first week in July. This is not necessarily a bad thing, but it is a confusing time. Summer has arrived like a great oceanliner calling into port, yet the days are already beginning to shorten. Up to this point, promise has underwritten all harvest and there has been a sense that there is still time to recover from setbacks and rectify mistakes, but from now on comes the realization that you reap only so much as you have sown. The phrase *next year* starts creeping into the gardener's vocabulary.

And yet, everything is filled right up to the brim. To regret the passing of these rich days is like mourning the anticipated aging of a child. The here-and-now is satisfying and demanding enough without starting to worry about its consequences.

July brings a number of harvests that confirm the whole point of growing seasonal foods in the garden. New potatoes, peas and soft fruit are all so much more delicious fresh from the garden than via the chilled industrial machinery of supermarket distribution that it is worth waiting most of the year for them. In the case of peas and potatoes, there is a simple chemical process that converts the sugar to starch in the first few hours after picking, so unless they are eaten at least the same day there is a real loss of sweetness. Soft fruit – strawberries, raspberries, gooseberries and currants – should be left unpicked until perfectly ripe to get the best taste. But at this stage they do not travel or keep at all well, so commercial varieties are invariably harvested before they are perfectly ripe. The result can be good but, if you have tasted the real thing, never good enough.

Any and every opportunity to eat outside is taken in summer and, by July, eating indoors feels the exception that defines the rule. Summer food needs to be eaten under a summer sun or, best of all, a round, full summer moon.

At the beginning of the month, sometime between midsummer and my birthday, I try to cut the orchard grass for the first time since the previous September. We let it grow mainly for the beauty of the grasses, especially in May and June, but also to deliberately impoverish the turf so that any wildflowers that want to establish themselves will not face overwhelming competition, which they would if the grass were regularly mown. Also, it saves work. The grass is long, dry and tough and takes about 10 hours to cut. A rotary mower will not cope with it at this length; I have done it on a number of occasions with a scythe, but that takes a couple of days. An Allen scythe or powered cutting blade is best. Cutting the grass is only half the job, as it all then has to be raked up, making huge piles of hay. I associate this with heat, sweat, itchy skin from the grass seed getting in one's clothes and a picnic tea sitting outside in the piles of grass. It is always a happy time.

We try to dig the first potatoes to celebrate my birthday on July 8. New potatoes take around 100 days from planting to harvest, so to achieve a good crop by this date they need to be planted at the end of March or beginning of April. The tubers are ready when the flowers appear and are fully open. They will go on swelling for as long as the haulms, or tops, remain green, but for new potatoes size is not an advantage. Anything much bigger than a marble is fair game. Digging a fork into the side of a ridge of the row and rummaging your fingers through the crumbly soil to feel the starchy nuggets is one of the great treats of the year. Unlike main-crop potatoes, which are harvested later, new potatoes always appear absurdly clean and pristine from the ground, as though already scrubbed. All they need is to be taken indoors, rinsed under a tap and put into boiling water until just tender. Rinse them and put them back into the pan with a few good-sized sprigs of applemint or spearmint (peppermint is not so good for cooking), plenty of butter or olive oil and some sea salt, then cover with a dry tea towel to absorb the steam. The first dish of new potatoes should be eaten unaccompanied, with the same respect normally reserved for asparagus or strawberries.

MONDAY, JULY 13:
Blight! Half potatoes blighted. Cut haulms, burned and earthed up.
Raking up yellow leaves off the damp soil was exactly like October.
Cold, wet, dying. But late evening was still lovely. Outside until 10 PM.

Here in Herefordshire we are very prone to potato blight. The commercial potato farmers spray against it every nine days. Blight is a fungal disease that hits the leaves, turning them yellow and killing them. The spores fall or are washed by rain to the ground and rain washes them into the potatoes, which then rot and quickly turn to a slimy, rotten mush with a characteristic, decomposing stench. The only solution is to cut off the top growth as soon as you notice the characteristic discoloration, rake up every shred of leaf and stem and burn them, and hope that the fungus has not reached the soil. This is a major pain but can save the day. Even if you save the crop – which we did – the potatoes stop growing from the moment the top growth is removed. So all the main crop – 'Rattle', 'Pink Fir Apple', 'Edzell Blue', 'Roseval', 'Kestrel' and 'Arran Victory' – remained very small. The earlies – 'BF15', 'Belle de Fontenay', 'Duke of York' and 'Ulster Chieftain' – were fine.

In an ideal world you do not store new potatoes, but dig and eat them as you need them. They keep as well in the ground as anywhere else. However, if you need the ground or are hit by blight, then they can be treated exactly as main-crop potatoes and all dug up and stored. Choose a dry day and dig them in the morning, leaving the potatoes on top of the soil to dry in the sun. Collect them at the end of the day

and store in a cool, dry, absolutely dark place. A paper or burlap sack is ideal. Plastic is no good, as the potatoes will sweat and rot. If stored like this, they should last until the following February or even March, when they are bound to start sprouting.

Fresh garlic, roasted as whole bulbs and eaten whole, is delicious, and the perfect accompaniment to spring lamb, which is killed in July. Once the tops start to die back in July, the bulbs beneath the soil will not grow anymore and are best dug up. They are often surprisingly deep and the ground has to be dug over deeply and carefully to get all the bulbs up.

To store well they need to be dried. The best way to do this is to leave them on the surface of the soil they have grown in, but only if the weather is dry. I use row covers over them, open at the ends, which I take off if there is no risk of rain. After a few days they can be gathered and the flaky outer skins removed before storing. Like onions, garlic

needs to be stored somewhere dry and cool but frost-free and preferably dark, although in the short term it will keep perfectly well for up to a month in the kitchen.

The garlic ground can then be dug over, a layer of mushroom compost forked in and either cabbages or zucchinis planted into it.

SUMMER PRUNING

The middle of July is the best time for summer pruning fruit trees. The purpose of this is to train and shape growth, whereas pruning when the plant is dormant in winter stimulates growth. Plums must only be pruned in summer, to do so in winter can cause them to ooze sap to such an extent that they "bleed" to death; for in general, they should only be pruned if damaged or growing intrusively.

Top fruit grown as espaliers, cordons and fans is therefore given a light pruning in midsummer, which stops any extravagant growth outside the desired shape and

allows light and air in to the growing fruit. I do not summer prune our orchard apples as yet, because they are too young to worry about. Their one annual pruning is in January or February. But the espaliered pears in the vegetable garden need cutting back and tying in to the cane supports. Pears fruit on spurs that have ripened (i.e., the wood that has hardened) the previous year, so the idea is to create healthy spurs for the crop that will be harvested in 15 months' time.

The first things to cut back are the improbably long, whippy new stems on each tree. Some of this will involve removing perfectly good, strong branches – which may be better than the existing framework, but in the wrong place. The lateral growth is then reduced by about a quarter and tied to the framework, and the spurs or vertical growth coming off the lateral branches are reduced to about 4 inches each in length.

The growing fruit is best thinned at this stage on both apples and pears. Too many small fruits crowded onto a branch will result in unripe, small fruits at harvesttime and, very possibly, broken branches. It is better to thin them so that each one has some space around it and so that there are not too many weighing down on potentially delicate young branches.

Opposite The espaliered pears before summer pruning. All the new vertical growth is cut back in July to three or four healthy buds that will provide next year's crop of pears. *Above* Peas, supported by hazel peasticks, ready for picking.

PEAS

Peas have to be eaten as fresh as possible, if not directly from the pod, to get their true sweetness. After a few hours the sugar starts to convert to starch and peas lose that magic. One of the enduring images of this garden is of our daughter Freya in the morning sun hidden among the rows of peas, picking them and eating them from the pod. Yet I do not remember her ever eating frozen peas. They are worth growing in the garden just so that the children can eat them raw and know what peas really taste like.

Peas have been grown domestically almost as long as wheat and were used primarily for their ability to be stored dried and then cooked to make a nutritious porridge. Shelling them and eating them fresh seems to have only begun in the sixteenth century, and to get their sweetness at its best you have to eat them when they are immature, with the pods just filling with the peas. This means picking over the lines of bushes almost daily, so it is important to leave enough room when you plant them to walk between the rows.

Modern pea breeding has concentrated on producing short-growing peas to make mechanized harvesting easier. But taller varieties take up no more space in the garden, are likely to ripen better and to crop more vigorously over a longer period. The only drawback to them is that they need supporting. 'Alderman' is a particularly tall variety, reaching over 6 feet in rich soil. But this is an advantage because height is always a virtue in the vegetable garden, adding a green texture and form that is much needed; even peasticks – the brushwood from hazel coppicing – look tremendous when staked out along the rows and have that wonderful mix of aesthetic beauty and completely functional purpose that a hedge has.

You can sow peas as early as October, along with the first fava beans, but we find it is best to wait until we sow our onion sets, which is likely to be the beginning of February. These will give an early picking in May, but if you are only making one or two sowings, anytime from the middle of March to the middle of May is fine. A good early variety is 'Feltham First' or 'Meteor'. 'Hurst Green Shaft' is a good pea for spring sowing, as is 'Kelvedon Wonder'. Purple-podded peas look wonderful on the bush, with rich purple pods hanging off the green leaves and tendrils, but I cannot honestly say that they taste any better than many other less good-looking varieties.

Snow peas and sugar snap peas are eaten whole, pods and all, and come in two forms, the flat ones, which are eaten before the peas grow, and the full ones (sugar snap), which have the swollen peas inside. Both are without the hard wall of the pod that conventional 'wrinkled' peas have. They are easy to cook and eat and are delicious but do not replace the pleasure of a bowl of young peas, freshly podded and lightly boiled before being eaten with good butter.

Peas dislike hot weather and grow best in the second half of spring, so a sowing after mid-May will not do well in a hot, dry year. They like lots of moisture but well-drained soil, so do best on a light soil that has been beefed up with plenty of organic compost. On our heavy clay the compost has the opposite effect, lightening it and improving drainage.

They can either be sown in drills a couple of inches deep in a single row with each pea spaced 2–3 inches apart or, as I do, in wider, flatter drills with twin rows spaced 4–5 inches apart. Each pair of rows should be 24 inches apart so that you have room to walk between them. Push the seeds lightly into the ground and then rake the soil back over them, marking the rows. It is important that the ground is perfectly weeded before you sow, because the peas will be difficult to weed once they are growing, although you can easily hoe between the rows. As long as they are staked, weeded and watered they will need no other care before eating them.

Pull the peas up when there are too few new pods being produced to make worthwhile pickings, fork the ground over and use it for winter brassicas or leeks.

About the same time as the early-sown peas are pulled up in July the French beans that were sown under cover can be planted out. I do this because our last few summers have

been so slug-ridden that if the beans are sown outside they get eaten off faster than they can grow, leaving stubs of stem in the ground. If planted out with strong root systems and decent-sized leaves they have a chance of outgrowing their attackers, although, in principle, it is much better to sow them direct.

GLOBE ARTICHOKES

Artichokes are the handsomest of all edible plants. We love the way they look so much (and the way that they taste) that we have lined a 100 foot path with flanking borders devoted to them. The huge, zigzagged leaves are a beautiful and surprisingly delicate glaucal gray for a plant that is so strong in outline. They certainly deserve their place in any flower border, whether you choose to harvest the flower heads for the table or not.

Although they start producing flower heads in May and continue right through to October, they are at their very best in July, when to go out on a summer's day filled with light and cut a basket of artichokes feels like living right.

As a food crop they are pretty undemanding, as long as you get their basic conditions right. They like sunshine, rich soil and good drainage. I have explained how to propagate them through offsets (see page 151) but they are also very easy to grow from seed. The seeds are large enough to handle individually and are ideally germinated in large plugs. I am sure that they would do best if sown directly where they were to grow, but our climate at Ivington is too unreliable for that, so I sow them in the greenhouse in April, potting them on from the plugs in May. They then spend a further month in their pots, which is long enough for the roots to develop, before being planted out. Artichokes are slow to develop and I have tried keeping them in pots until they start to grow more vigorously. But it is better to put them in the ground, where they will sulk and not do much until midsummer. Growth will come

they will do in a few weeks, repeat the process with the other half. In a mild year mint will not die back until November, and starts to grow again in early spring.

ROSEMARY

As well as freshly harvested garlic, spring lamb must have rosemary. Given the right conditions, rosemary is terribly easy to grow, and to provide those conditions all you have to do is think of stony Mediterranean scrub. Of all the herbs, rosemary is happiest on poor, dry soil. All it needs is sun and good drainage. It is not fully hardy and can be killed by extreme frosts but as long as it is not cold and wet at the same time, it is likely to survive most northern weather. When planting rosemary, dig the hole deeply and remove the topsoil. We replace the subsoil with stones and fine gravel and use the subsoil to plant the rosemary into. If the soil is too rich you get very soft, sappy growth that is much more vulnerable to the cold. Rosemary is evergreen and can

be cut all year round, but is much more aromatically pungent when its oil is heated by sunshine. It will not regenerate from old wood so do not cut back too hard, but keep cutting evenly from all over the plant to encourage fresh growth.

We grow only two varieties, the ordinary *Rosmarinus officinalis* and the cultivar 'Miss Jessopp'. As far as taste goes, I cannot tell the difference between the two, but the ordinary *R. officinalis* has much more sprawling, gangly growth, as opposed to the prim and upright 'Miss Jessopp'.

Rosemary will grow from seed sown in spring but it is easier to take cuttings in late summer, putting them in a compost that is 50 percent gravel or perlite. Water the cuttings sparingly for the first few weeks and keep them dry over winter. They should be ready to pot on in spring, planting them out when the roots have established and they are growing strongly in early summer.

STRAWBERRIES

The strawberry has been perverted in my lifetime. What was once a seasonal, richly sensual treat has become a year-round commonplace, the pulpy, tasteless fruit not worth its place in the kitchen. Which is not to say that strawberries are not delicious or should not be grown, but simply to show the difference between fresh, properly produced fruit and commercial rubbish.

For a start, strawberries should never be eaten cold. This completely flattens their taste. The best strawberries are eaten in the garden picked directly from the plant while warm from the sun. Secondly, they need to be eaten only when absolutely ripe. Picked too soon, the sugar content has not sufficiently developed, and overripe they are sickly.

Summer strawberries should ideally be planted in September in a sunny site in rich, well-prepared soil, allowing 24 inches each way between plants. If planted in winter or spring, the flowers should be removed when they appear to let the plant develop so that a good crop can be picked the subsequent year. The spring after planting they must be kept weed-free, watered in dry weather and mulched with compost in early spring and then with something to keep the strawberries dry and clean from early summer. Traditionally, straw was used, but this can encourage slugs. Slugs and birds are the two biggest enemies of strawberries, and whereas netting will deter most birds, slugs are more difficult to stop. The fruit is picked as it ripens.

Each plant will put out runners, which can be pinned to the ground to produce new plants. When these have established roots – which they will do in a few weeks and can be seen by new growth – cut the runners on either side, dig them up and transplant.

Strawberry plants are at their most productive for only about four years, so ideally you should establish a new group in a separate plot each year, with the first year producing nothing, the next three years very productive, and the plants put on the compost heap at the end of the fourth summer. This is putting too high a value on the fruits. The only certain rule is not to replant a cleared site with strawberries again. Use it for another crop for a few years to avoid any risk of virus diseases.

Alpine, or wild, strawberries are in many ways a better fruit. Plant them in spring or autumn and they are absurdly easy to grow – in fact, they can become a weed – and provide wonderful miniature strawberries from midsummer right up until the first frosts. Although they will grow in complete shade and on poor soil, the fruits are best in sunshine. I remember hunting out wild strawberries in the hedgerows as a child, and greedily gobbling up the honey-sweet, pea-sized fruits. Even in the garden it takes quite a bit of picking to collect a bowl, so they are best used for grazing on while weeding. But nonetheless wonderful for that.

CURRANTS

Blackcurrants are quite different from red- or whitecurrants. The latter two, however, are simply different-colored versions of the same fruit. But all currants are plants of woodland margins, so they like some light shade and a rich, moist soil. Blackcurrants, in particular, thrive on rich conditions, whereas red- and whitecurrants will grow almost anywhere and survive almost any amount of maltreatment.

In practice, it makes sense to grow all three types of currants, raspberries and gooseberries together, as they share the same broad requirements and all need to be protected from birds. A fruit cage of some sort, be it an elaborate creation or temporary netting supported by canes, is therefore a necessity.

All currants should be planted in autumn or winter in soil that has been well dug and manured. The richer the soil the better the crop will be, and blackcurrants should be given the most protected, richest part of the site if that choice has to be made.

The most significant difference between blackcurrants and the others is in the pruning regime. Red- and whitecurrants fruit on spurs produced on old wood – rather like apples and pears – and therefore must be pruned back primarily to keep them open and healthy and also to reduce new wood by about a half. Blackcurrants produce fruit on new wood, with the best fruit being produced on wood a year old. Therefore they are usually pruned down to the ground every third year. There are two ways of doing this: You either hard-prune one-third of each plant every year, or prune one-third of your bushes completely every year. The net effect is the same.

RASPBERRIES

A bowl of fresh raspberries, eaten with light cream, is always incomparably better than any strawberry. Raspberries do not travel well, so fresh ones from your own garden will always be better than any cultivated commercially, which will be a variety especially chosen for its durability rather than its taste.

There are two kinds of raspberries, summer-fruiting and autumn-fruiting. Summer raspberries fruit from late June through August, which is when the earliest autumn-fruiting

ones begin cropping, going through until November. Summer-fruiting raspberries fruit on canes grown the previous year, while autumn ones crop on canes grown the same year.

This obviously affects the pruning regime, so for summer ones you prune the canes that have just finished fruiting right back to the ground, leaving an evenly spaced selection of strong new canes that have grown that year to ripen off ready to fruit next year. Autumn raspberries are cut back to the ground in winter or early spring and the new growth will provide fruit nine months later. We grow 'Glen Moy' for summer and 'Autumn Bliss' for autumn harvest.

For summer pudding you need summer-fruiting raspberries, but autumn-fruiting varieties often have better flavor and are much less likely to be attacked by birds, so do not need to be grown in a fruit cage. Summer raspberries can be grown in some shade, whereas autumn ones will do better in a sunny site. Both should be planted in winter, with plenty of manure added to the ground. They like lots of moisture but must have good drainage – and that combination is best created by plenty of organic matter in the ground. Raspberries dislike being moved. They will grow perfectly well against a fence, and in a small garden this may be the best position for them, as long as you make sure that they get a really good soak at least once a week. Normally, they are grown against wires fixed horizontally between strong posts so that they can be tied in.

The best raspberries are grown around Blairgowrie in Scotland, because the climate and soil are exactly right. They like a cool, wet summer with a light, slightly acidic soil reinforced with plenty of muck. They have shallow roots that need heavy mulching every year to feed them and to keep the roots cool, and to keep them weed-free.

THE FLOWER GARDEN

There is always a big bunch of flowers from the garden on the kitchen table and while vegetables, fruit and herbs are a major part of our garden, they are by no means all of it or even the most important part. The real heart of the garden is an area right in the center that we call the jewel garden. It is a theme reflecting the 10 years we spent working together as jewelers and the idea is for it to have the richness and intensity of a box of jewels.

The 82 x 82 foot area is subdivided into 16 square beds with two crossing central paths and much smaller cruciform access paths. We use yellow and gold flowers and leaves to represent gold, which include trees such as *Robinia* and laburnum, *Achillea*, potentillas and thalictrums. Silver is represented by the glaucal foliage of weeping pears, cardoons, *Macleaya*, *Melianthus*, *Stachys byzantina* and grasses such as *Festuca glauca* and *Helictotrichon sempervirens*.

We have learned that everything must be planted in large blocks, sometimes with as many as seven plants in a group, to get the intensity of effect. In among these polished facets of color one can dot strong magentas, oranges and lime greens that have the power to survive dissipation without being diminished.

The other thing that is essential applies to any kind of planting, and that is that the color of flowers is only as effective as the foliage that backs the flowers. So we use the full range of leaves from the jet straps of *Ophiopogon* 'Nigrescens' through all the hundred greens, the bronze and straw-colored grasses, to the purple and ruby leaves of purple hazel, orache – which is delicious to eat and has seeded itself from its original sowing in the vegetable garden – and the burgundy cow parsley *Anthriscus sylvestris* 'Ravenswing'.

The rich jewel colors come from a range of plants, such as *Penstemon* 'Garnet', *Angelica gigas*, *Dianthus barbatus*, Oriental poppies, the rich plum color of opium poppies, salvias (especially *Salvia guaranitica*), the dahlia 'Bishop of Llandaff', *Geum* 'Mrs Bradshaw', *Knautia macedonica*, chocolate cosmos *(Cosmos atrosanguineus)*, delphiniums, sweet Williams, tithonias, sunflowers, leonotis, alliums, crocosmia and clematis on tripods such as *C. viticella*

'Purpurea Plena Elegans', *C. jackmanii*, and *C.* 'Etoile Violette', as well as dozens of tripods smothered with sweet peas. An indispensable foil that seeds itself everywhere is *Verbena bonariensis*, which provides a backing purple from August through to November.

There are no white flowers and the only pale colors come from foliage. Ideally, you should feel as though you are inside the jewel, submerged by intense color rather than looking on with polite botanical curiosity.

FRIDAY, JULY 17:

Kitchen garden feels abandoned, sprawly, bare and amateurish. New vegetable bit has simple charm but little to it yet.

The wind has slowed all growth down. Place is retarded and scruffy and thoroughly below par.

Garden lost really – but always the case at this time of year. This is No Man's Land.

ARTICHOKES WITH BEURRE BLANC

You can eat artichokes whole simply with olive oil and salt, or a classic beurre blanc. This is best using the variety 'Green Globe', which grows well in England. It is gloriously messy, and the table is littered with remains like a Roman feast.

2 lemons, cut in half

1 sprig of fresh bay leaves

6 large artichokes or 12 small ones

For the beurre blanc

8 shallots, finely sliced

6 tablespoons dry white wine

6 tablespoons white wine vinegar

8 oz unsalted butter

½ lemon

Sea salt and pepper

Serves 6

Have a large pan of boiling salted water ready. Add the halved lemons and the bay to the water. The lemon prevents discoloration of the artichokes.

Prepare the artichokes by trimming the stalk, leaving 1–2 inches, and shaking out any earwigs. I do no other preparation. As fast as possible, put the artichokes into the pan of boiling water and cook for about 30 minutes. You can check to see if they are cooked when one of the outer leaves can be pulled easily away.

To make the beurre blanc, put the shallots in a pan with the wine and the vinegar and boil together until the liquid has reduced by half. Cut the butter into cubes, and whisk the pieces one at a time into the shallots over a low heat, until you have a creamy sauce. Add a squeeze of lemon juice, season and serve immediately, or keep warm over a double boiler if necessary.

STRAWBERRY TART

A simple tart covered in fresh fruit looks lovely and summery. Raspberries would be just as good instead of strawberries. You can make the tart base and the custard in advance, ready for assembly and baking. To prevent a skin from forming as the custard cools, cover it with a thin layer of sifted powdered sugar.

½ recipe Sweet Pastry (see page 146)

8 oz strawberries

For the custard

3 large egg yolks

2 ½ oz golden caster sugar or granulated sugar

½ vanilla pod

1 heaping teaspoon unbleached plain flour

½ cup milk

½ cup heavy cream

Serves 8

Oven temperature: 375°F

FROM THE GARDEN TO THE TABLE

Line a 12 inch baking pan with the pastry. Prick well and bake unfilled for 10–15 minutes until slightly colored.

Whisk the egg yolks and sugar until they are light and frothy. Cut open the vanilla pod, scrape out the soft black insides with a teaspoon and mix in with the eggs. Sift the flour and add to the mixture. Warm the milk and cream together to body temperature – test with your finger. Pour the milk and cream into the egg mixture a little at a time, whisking continuously. Return to the pan, and gently bring to a boil, stirring all the time. Boil for a couple of minutes, then allow to cool.

Spread the custard over the pastry and bake for 15–20 minutes with a piece of parchment paper or aluminum foil over to protect the surface of the custard.

Wait for it to become cold, then slice the strawberries lengthwise and pack them closely over the surface of the tart. Serve immediately.

LAVENDER SHORTBREAD

I rarely make biscuits, but these are unusual and are good for tea or with ice cream or sorbet. The rice flour makes them lighter in texture. They are at their best stored in a tin for 24 hours before eating, so the slight bitterness from the aromatic oils is reduced.

4 oz unsalted butter

2 oz caster or granulated sugar, plus extra for sprinkling

4 oz unbleached plain flour

2 oz fine rice flour

1 teaspoon lavender flowers

1 teaspoon finely chopped lavender leaves

Makes 12–20 (depending on the size of the cutter)

Oven temperature: 300°F

Cream the butter and the sugar together, then stir in the flour, rice flour and lavender flowers and leaves. You can make this in a food processor, but don't add the lavender

and leaves until the last few seconds so they don't get too chopped up.

Roll out the dough on a floured surface to about ¼ inch thick, and cut into biscuits of whatever shape you like. Transfer to a baking tray lined with nonstick parchment. Bake in the preheated oven for 20 minutes. Sprinkle with sugar, then cool on a wire rack.

ICE CREAM

Homemade ice cream is foolproof made in an inexpensive ice cream maker. This recipe is a rich treat, like Cornish vanilla ice cream used to be. It is fantastic with raspberries or simply alone.

6 large egg yolks

5 oz caster or granulated sugar

1 vanilla pod, split open

16 fl oz whole milk

½ pint heavy cream

Serves 6

Whisk the egg yolks and sugar together in a bowl.

Scrape the inner black sticky seeds from the vanilla pod, and add to the milk in a saucepan. Heat the milk to just below the boiling point, then let stand off the heat for about 5 minutes to develop the flavor of the vanilla.

Pour the milk over the eggs and sugar, whisking continuously. Return to the heat in a double boiler, and stir with a wooden spoon until thickened. Be careful not to overheat, or the mixture will separate into grainy lumps. Allow the mixture to cool, then stir in the cream.

Put into your ice cream maker and freeze churn according to the manufacturer's instructions.

SUMMER PUDDING

One of the greatest treats of the gastronomic year is summer pudding. The combination of white bread, red- and blackcurrants and raspberries does not at first strike one as that special, but it is one of those combinations of ingredients that is sublimely right. A good summer pudding – and such a thing cannot be bought over any counter and is very rarely served in any restaurant – is a wonderful thing.

The first thing that everyone agrees on is that no one agrees on the correct mix of ingredients. But you must have blackcurrants, raspberries and redcurrants in some proportion. Strawberries ruin it. They have the wrong texture and a blandness that spoils that particularly rich tartness of the pudding. Always serve with cream. Organic heavy cream is best.

14 oz raspberries
10 oz blackcurrants
10 oz redcurrants
5 oz caster or granulated sugar
8 slices day-old white bread
Serves 6

Pick over the raspberries and put them in a large bowl.

Stem and tail the currants. To release their juices, cook the blackcurrants and redcurrants separately in saucepans with half the sugar in each and just enough water to prevent them from burning. Simmer for 2 minutes. Add the hot currants to the raspberries, and mix them all together.

Use a 5½-cup pudding bowl. Cut a circle of bread for the bottom, and line the sides by overlapping the slices to cover completely. Pack the bowl with the fruit and juice, keeping back a little of the juice. Put another circle of bread on to cover the top. Cover with a plate with a weight and leave in the refrigerator for 24 hours.

Turn out onto a plate. Pour the reserved juice over any white patches of bread.

RASPBERRY JAM

This is the most popular jam with the children. I don't mind if it is a little runnier than storebought jam. You cook it very quickly so it doesn't lose its brilliant color and fresh taste.

3 lb 3 oz caster or granulated sugar
3 lb 3 oz raspberries
Makes six to seven 1 lb jars
Oven temperature: 300°F

Spread the sugar on a baking tray and warm it gently for about 20 minutes in the preheated oven to help it dissolve quickly when you add it to the fruit.

Pick over the raspberries and place in a large saucepan. Warm over a gentle heat for 30 minutes.

Stir the raspberries – as you do this some of the berries will be crushed and their juice will run. Add the warm sugar and continue to cook, stirring gently until the sugar has all dissolved. Bring it to a boil and boil for 5 minutes.

Take the pan off the heat, and test a drop of jam on a cold saucer for set: Leave it for a few seconds to cool, then push the jam with your finger – the surface should wrinkle. If necessary, boil for a little longer and keep testing it.

Pour into warm, sterilized jam jars, and place a waxed disc on the surface. When cooled, cover with a cellophane cover and rubber band.

AUGUST

AUGUST HAS A RANGE of nonhorticultural and culinary associations that nevertheless load themselves onto the garden. It is the school vacation and, between the ages of 7 and 17, I went away to school at the beginning of May and did not see the garden again until the end of July. We would step out of school summer into home summer – so just being at home in the garden in August was a vacation. And this split summer is a useful divide for the garden. There is a real change sometime around the middle to end of July that is always complete by August. Although all the youth and spring has gone out of the garden's step, it is now a rich place, confidently cruising through the days.

But the nights are growing noticeably shorter and cooler, and the way in which the garden is growing changes too. Many of the early-summer crops like fava beans, peas and spinach have to be cleared and the ground used for winter crops that have been grown on in a seedbed or pots. It is the time to plant out all the cabbages, broccoli and leeks that will be ready for harvest in the New Year. Zucchinis, all kinds of lettuce, French and runner beans, new potatoes, indoor tomatoes, cucumbers, carrots, beets, onions, shallots and spring-sown parsley are all being harvested daily.

There is an element of tyranny in this – if you do not keep picking small amounts regularly everything quickly goes to seed or gets unpalatably big before you are ready to eat it. This is where experience of successional sowing really comes into play, so that you have enough mature plants to give you the luxury of choice and selection when you want it within each type of vegetable, but also others

coming through to provide waves of harvest. Earlier in the year there is a tendency to grow as much as possible and to fill the ground, but from the beginning of August into October the secret is to grow enough but not too much, and the time to plan and put that into effect is in May and June.

Any suitable day during the last two weeks of August is an excellent time to sow seeds for autumn eating, like rocket, lettuce, chicory, spinach, corn salad, parsley and mizuna, as well as spring greens, Swiss chard, onions and winter purslane for eating next spring. The ground is still warm and yet the cooler nights allow plants like lettuce – which is reluctant to germinate above 68°F – the chance to grow steadily without bolting. The cool night air also causes dew, which plays a significant role in watering seedlings. Weeds, too, like August and the extent to which you keep on top of them and do not let them seed will largely influence the extent of the weeding that you have to do next spring.

The long grass in the orchard is not cut until midsummer, and then it is all raked up and piled into three or four great haystacks. The grass is bone dry and you can pitch great mounds of it onto the end of a hay fork, although inevitably you get covered in hay and grass seed in the process. It is hard but lovely work and the hay makes a good mulch for hedges and fruit trees.

For most of the late-summer or autumn crops, like tomatoes, squashes, sweet corn and zucchinis, this is the critical period when lack of sun and heat will determine the speed and extent of ripening before the weather runs out in October. Little things can make a big difference. So, for example, I always strip off all lower leaves on the tomatoes and any shading the fruit from the sun, which not only improves ripening but increases ventilation as well, preventing fungal attacks — which tomatoes are prone to on our heavy soil.

The globe artichokes suffer no such problems, nor do we mind that they produce more heads than we can eat, because they look so wonderful. In late spring we eat them whole, when the flower heads are the size of a brussels sprout, cutting them into quarters and frying them; but now, in late summer, they are large and best eaten scale by scale, dipped in butter or beurre blanc made from freshly harvested shallots.

BEETS

Although baby carrots and beets can be pulled from early June in a good year, August is really the month when the root crops start to provide a reliable harvest. Young beets are particularly good at this stage and lovely roasted with thyme and fresh garlic, made into soup or served with hot cream.

Beets are terribly easy to grow, needing neither particularly rich conditions nor exceptional weather, but they do not like soggy, wet soil and do best in a sunny position on light soil that has been manured the previous year. A little beet goes quite a long way, so I make just two sowings from each packet; if one is a disaster, it hardly matters.

We grow 'Boltardy', 'Detroit 2 Tardel' and 'Chioggia'. The seeds are corky and quite big so it is worth the trouble of spacing them carefully about 2 inches apart. These will then be thinned initially to twice that distance and, thereafter, pickings made to thin those that are left rather

than starting at the end of a row and working down it systematically. First sowings can be made in March and April for using in summer and in July for winter usage. The tops can be cooked like chard leaves — the two plants are very closely related.

ONIONS

"To know one's onions" (meaning that one has a sure grasp of what is going on) implies that "knowing" onions is a complex and difficult thing to do. They are certainly a very varied family and there are many different types, although all onions share similar basic characteristics.

Bulb onions (*Allium cepa*) and the rest of the allium family (garlic, leeks, shallots and chives) have been a mainstay of the kitchen garden here for at least 1,000 years, given that there has been a house here for that long and we can be reasonably certain that there would always have been a garden of some kind for growing vegetables and herbs. We know that when the current building was erected in the fifteenth century, scallions, chibol and holekes were being used, and that scallions were used green and the latter two were dried and grown from seed or sets like our modern onion.

Scallions may also have referred to Welsh onions. Spring onions, by the way, did not reach Britain until the eighteenth century. We grow Welsh onions, whose bulbs are produced not underground, like most of the family, but at the ends of their leaves. As the bulbs swell, the weight of them bends the leaf over until it touches the ground, where the bulb will root. *Welsh* does not refer to Wales but is from the Old German *welsch*, meaning "foreign." Their qualities, other than the purely culinary, included serving: "to provoke and stirre folk to the act of carnal copulation, and to have a good appetite."

If knowing one's onions is complicated, growing one's onions is very straightforward. You simply encourage them to swell until they will swell no more. A combination of rich, well-drained soil, water, weeding and thinning will do this. Onion sets, baby onions about the size of crocus bulbs, are a lot easier than seeds to grow but to nurture onions from a tiny black seed, via a wispy, grasslike seedling to one of those opulent globes, is far more satisfying.

Onions sown in April have done as much growing as they can and will now either sprout, using up the reserves of their bulb, which is all an onion is, or else rot in the wet. They are therefore ready to lift and store. Onions can be dried on the soil where they grew or on a path, but it is easier to lift them and store them on racks in the potting shed where the air can dry them and they are protected from the rain.

They have been weeded weekly, and thinned two or three times so that they have room to grow and are not fighting for nutrients, although I do not thin our onions as much as many books recommend. It is not size that we are judging them by but taste and convenience in the kitchen. We want medium-sized bulbs that will be used up in one dish rather than the mammoth specimens of fevered male horticultural imagination, which so often hang guiltily around the fridge in various stages of division until they are thrown away unused.

We tend to think of onions as intrinsically encased in a dried-up shell. But a newly dug onion has the juicy freshness of an apple. This demands urgent eating as though, like new potatoes, there might be something to be lost in the storage.

To get the essential sweetness of an onion they must be roasted whole. Nothing could be simpler. Do not skin, cut or trim them, just rub off any soil with your hands, put them onto a baking tray and stick them in a hot oven for an hour or so. They are done when you can slide a fork into the middle. The charred outer layers act as a casing, which you break open to reveal the soft, inner flesh. Obviously, the bigger the onion the longer it takes to cook, but if you roast them too small you lose the lovely and slightly absurd sight of a whole onion exactly as it has been lifted from the garden onto your plate.

GARLIC

Garlic grows very well at this northerly latitude but needs a very long growing season to mature, so we plant the cloves whenever conditions are right between mid-October and Christmas. The roots grow and the bulbs shoot and grow on in mild weather but can stop growing for a month at a time if it is very cold. This does not matter. The important thing is that the plant has a long time to establish large bulbs with well-determined cloves.

There is a school of thought that says northern gardeners should use cloves from bulbs grown in latitudes similar to their own so that they are adjusted to the climate, but we have grown very successful crops from garlic bought in the south of France without any problems of adjustment. The one certain rule is that the garlic you harvest will only be as good as the garlic you plant, so always use large, healthy cloves.

The ground wants to be deeply dug, with plenty of compost added, and in full sun. The site of the previous season's bean crop is ideal. Plant each clove individually with the most pointed end upward, fully 1 inch below the surface. As a rule of thumb, I consider the soil not to be prepared thoroughly enough if you cannot push the cloves easily in with your finger. Plant them in either rows or blocks, with 9 inches between each clove. Rake gently over. There is nothing more to be done save to keep them well weeded, as with all allium crops, and to harvest them when the leaves start to yellow and die down. Harvest them during a period of fine, dry weather, digging the bulbs up carefully – they are soft and easily bruised at this stage – and leave them lying on the surface of the soil for a few days to dry out. The drier they are, the longer they will keep.

But take some of the crop for eating now, as roasted whole bulbs of fresh garlic are deliciously sweet, with none of the bitter pungency it develops as it dries. When the bulbs have dried out, peel off the loose, dry skin and any rotten leaves and store them in a dark, frost-free place tied in ropes or on racks so that air can circulate around them.

Above When you first lift 'Red Brunswick' onions they have a glossy sheen and look more like a polished apple than an onion. Exposure to the air soon dulls this into a protective matte opacity. *Right* Garlic bulbs are planted deeper than onions and have to be dug up with a fork. They often emerge encrusted with soil, which has to be rubbed off to reveal the swollen bulb at the base.

SUNDAY, AUGUST 23:

Very wet and blustery all day.

Bought seeds and potting compost.

*Sowed three trays of spring cabbage. Trimmed off side
leaves of celeriac.*

*Wheelbarrowed two loads of manure to activate compost.
Cut comfrey for it.*

*Sowed seed trays of beets, mixed salad leaves and
carrots.*

Watered slug-eating nematodes into vegetable garden.

BEET SOUP

This soup is a deep wine red, and it is so simple to make.
Try to choose even-sized beets so they cook at the same
rate.

1 lb 5 oz whole beets

1 large onion, finely chopped

½ oz butter

3 cups chicken or vegetable stock

2 tablespoons cream or crème fraîche

Serves 6

Don't stem and tail the beets, just wash them thoroughly,
leaving the root and 2 inches of leaves intact. Put into a pan
of cold water and bring to a boil. Simmer for at least 30
minutes – older beets later in the season will take longer.
They are ready when the skin wrinkles and rubs off easily.
Drain.

When they are cool enough to handle, rub the skins off
and roughly chop the beets.

Cook the onion gently in the butter without browning.
Add the beets and the stock and heat it all together.

Process the soup until it is smooth.

Reheat, season and serve with a dollop of cream or
crème fraîche and a sprinkle of chives on each bowl.

ROAST BEETS WITH THYME AND GARLIC

Beets can be roasted, as here, or boiled whole, with the
leafy stalks left on and the root and skin intact. If boiling,
cook until the skin rubs off easily, which can take anything
from 20 minutes to 1½ hours, depending upon the size and
age of the beets. Roasting is a quicker way to cook them.

6 even-sized small beets

3 small whole heads garlic, each cut in half horizontally

Large bunch of fresh thyme

Sea salt

Olive oil

Serves 6

Oven temperature: 375°F

Wash the beets and chop off leafy tops, leaving the skin
intact. Quarter, and arrange in a roasting dish surrounded by
the garlic heads cut in half. Scatter over the thyme and sea
salt, and drizzle with olive oil. Turn the beets in the oil to
ensure that all surfaces are coated. Roast in the preheated
oven for 35–40 minutes. Serve hot, with the garlic.

BEETS WITH SALTY CREAM

This raises beets to the culinary heights, and works well
with any roast meat.

12 small or 6 medium (tennis-ball-sized) beets

18 fl oz heavy cream

Sea salt

Serves 6

Oven temperature: 450°F

Don't stem and tail the beets, just wash them thoroughly,
leaving the root and 2 inches of leaves intact. Put into a pan
of cold water and bring to a boil. Simmer for about 30
minutes – older beets will take longer. They are ready when
the skin wrinkles and rubs off easily. Drain.

When they are cool enough to handle, rub the skins off. Put them in an ovenproof dish where they will fit snugly in one layer. Pour over the heavy cream and sprinkle liberally with salt. Bake in the preheated oven for about 20 minutes. The cream turns into a gaudy pink sauce.

FRIED CUCUMBERS

A simple salad of raw, finely sliced cucumbers dressed with oil, vinegar and salt doesn't need a recipe. When we have a glut this is a rich and unusual way of using cucumbers as a hot dish. It goes well with roast chicken and has a delicate summery lightness.

1 large cucumber (or 2 small ones)
1 oz butter
2 tablespoons heavy cream
Sea salt
1 tablespoon finely chopped fresh summer savory
Serves 6

Peel the cucumber and cut lengthwise into 4 inch long fingers. Don't cut them too small or they will lose their shape in cooking.

Fry the cucumber in the butter in a large frying pan until lightly browned – about 10 minutes. Stir in the heavy cream and season.

Add the herbs just before serving.

GRILLED LEG OF LAMB WITH HERBS

We are fortunate enough to have grazing rights on a common near the house, and keep a couple of lambs each year to fatten for our own use. When we had a power outage one weekend we had to cook a meal over the open fire in the kitchen. Instead of roasting the lamb in the oven, it was boned first and marinated so that it would cook quickly on a rack over the fire. This works perfectly well on a barbecue or under a grill.

1 leg of lamb, about 4–5 lbs
Sea salt and pepper
For the marinade
4 cloves garlic
4 tablespoons chopped fresh rosemary
Bunch of fresh thyme
4 tablespoons olive oil
2 tablespoons wine vinegar or the juice of 1 lemon
Serves 6–8

Bone and butterfly the leg (or a butcher will do this for you), and remove any excess fat and the skin. (I'm fussy about the way raw meat looks – it should be carefully dressed to make it look appetizing.) Roughly chop the garlic and the rosemary, then rub them into the meat. Mix the thyme, olive oil and vinegar or lemon juice and pour over the meat. Marinate the meat for several hours – it can be left overnight in the refrigerator.

Cook the meat under a preheated very hot grill, or on a barbecue, searing it quickly first on both sides before letting it cook for about 10 minutes on each side, depending upon how pink you like it, and the temperature of the barbecue or grill. Season before serving. The crusty dark outside, fragrant with herbs, contrasts beautifully with the succulent pink meat inside and tastes fantastic. This is what being a carnivore is all about.

Food always tastes better when it is eaten outside on a warm evening, with garden torches lighting the growing darkness. A boned leg of organic lamb, raised on the water meadow butting onto the garden, strewn with plenty of rosemary and cooked over the most basic of wood fires, is not sophisticated cuisine, but a genuine feast nevertheless.

INDEX

Page numbers in *italic* refer to illustrations.

U.S. SEED SUPPLIERS

Burgess Plant and Seed Co.
905 Four Seasons Road
Bloomington, IL 61701
(309) 663-9551

W. Atlee Burpee & Co.
300 Park Avenue
Warminster, PA 18974
(800) 888-1447

The Cook's Garden
PO Box 535
Londonderry, VT 05148
(800) 457-9703/Fax (800) 457-9705

Johnny's Selected Seeds
310 Foss Hill Road
Albion, ME 04910-9731
(207) 437-4301/Fax (800) 437-4290

Kitchen Garden Seeds
23 Tulip Drive
Bantam, CT 06750
(860) 567-6086/Fax (860) 567-5323

Pinetree Garden Seeds
PO Box 300
New Gloucester, ME 04260
(207) 926-3400/Fax (207) 926-3886

Ronniger's
Star Route "B"
Moyie Springs, ID 83845
(208) 267-7938/Fax (208) 267-3265
(Over sixty varieties of seed potatoes)

Seed Savers Exchange
3076 North Winn Road
Decorah, IA 52101
(563) 382-5990

Seeds of Change
PO Box 15700
Santa Fe, NM 87506-5700
(505) 438-8080/Fax (505) 438-7052
(Heirloom vegetables – all organically grown)

Shepherd's Garden Seeds
30 Irene Street
Torrington, CT 06790
(203) 482-3638/California (408) 335-6910
(Wide selection of common and exotic vegetables)

Thompson & Morgan Seed Catalogue
PO Box 1308
Jackson, NJ 08527-0308
(800) 274-7333

Tomato Growers Supply Co.
PO Box 2237
Fort Myers, FL 33902
(888) 478-7333/Fax (888) 768-3476
(Good variety of tomatoes and peppers)

Totally Tomatoes
PO Box 1626
Augusta, GA 30903
(803) 663-0016/Fax (888) 477-7333
(Specializes in tomatoes and peppers)

Vermont Bean Seed Co.
Garden Lane
Fair Haven, VT 05743
(803) 663-0217/Fax (888) 500-7333
(Good selection of beans)

Vesey's Seeds
Box 9000
Calais, ME 04619
(902) 368-7333/Fax (902) 566-1620
(Vegetables, herbs, and flowers for the short season garden)

U.S. FRUIT TREE SUPPLIERS

Big Horse Creek Farm
PO Box 70
Lansing, NC 28643
(336) 384-1134

Burnt Ridge Nursery
432 Burnt Ridge
Onalaska, WA 98570
(360) 985-2873/Fax (360) 985-0882

Cumberland Valley Nurseries Inc.
PO Box 471
McMinnville, TN 37110-0471
(800) 492-0022/Fax (615) 473-4279

Edible Landscaping
PO Box 77
Afton, VA 22920
(804) 361-9134/Fax (804) 361-1916

Hilltop Nurseries
PO Box 578, 60895 CR 681
Hartford, MI 49057
(800) 253-2511

Just Fruits
Route 2 Box 4818
Crawfordville, FL 32327
(904) 926-5644

Mellinger's
2310 W. South Range Road
North Lima, OH 44452-9731
(800) 321-7444

Nolin River Nut Tree Nursery
797 Port Wooden Road
Upton, KY 42784
(270) 369-8551

Oikos Tree Crops
PO Box 19425
Kalamazoo, MI 49019-0425
(616) 624-6233

Raintree Nursery
391 Butts Road
Morton, WA 98356
(360) 496-6400/Fax (888) 770-8358

Womack Nursery Co.
2551 Hwy 6
DeLeon, TX 76444-9631
(254) 893-6497/Fax (254) 893-3400